corinne maier - anne simon

MARX

an illustrated biography

NOBROW

LONDON - NEW YORK

Thank you to Pauline Mermet

Marx © DARGAUD 2013, by Simon, Maier
www.dargaud.com
This is a first English edition printed in 2014 by Nobrow Ltd.
62 Great Eastern Street, London, EC2A 3QR.
Corinne Maier and Anne Simon have asserted their right under the Copyright,
Designs and Patents Act, 1988, to be identified as the author and illustrator of this Work.
Published in the US by Nobrow (US) inc.
Printed in Poland on FSC assured paper.
iSBN: 978-1-907704-83-3

Order from www.nobrow.net

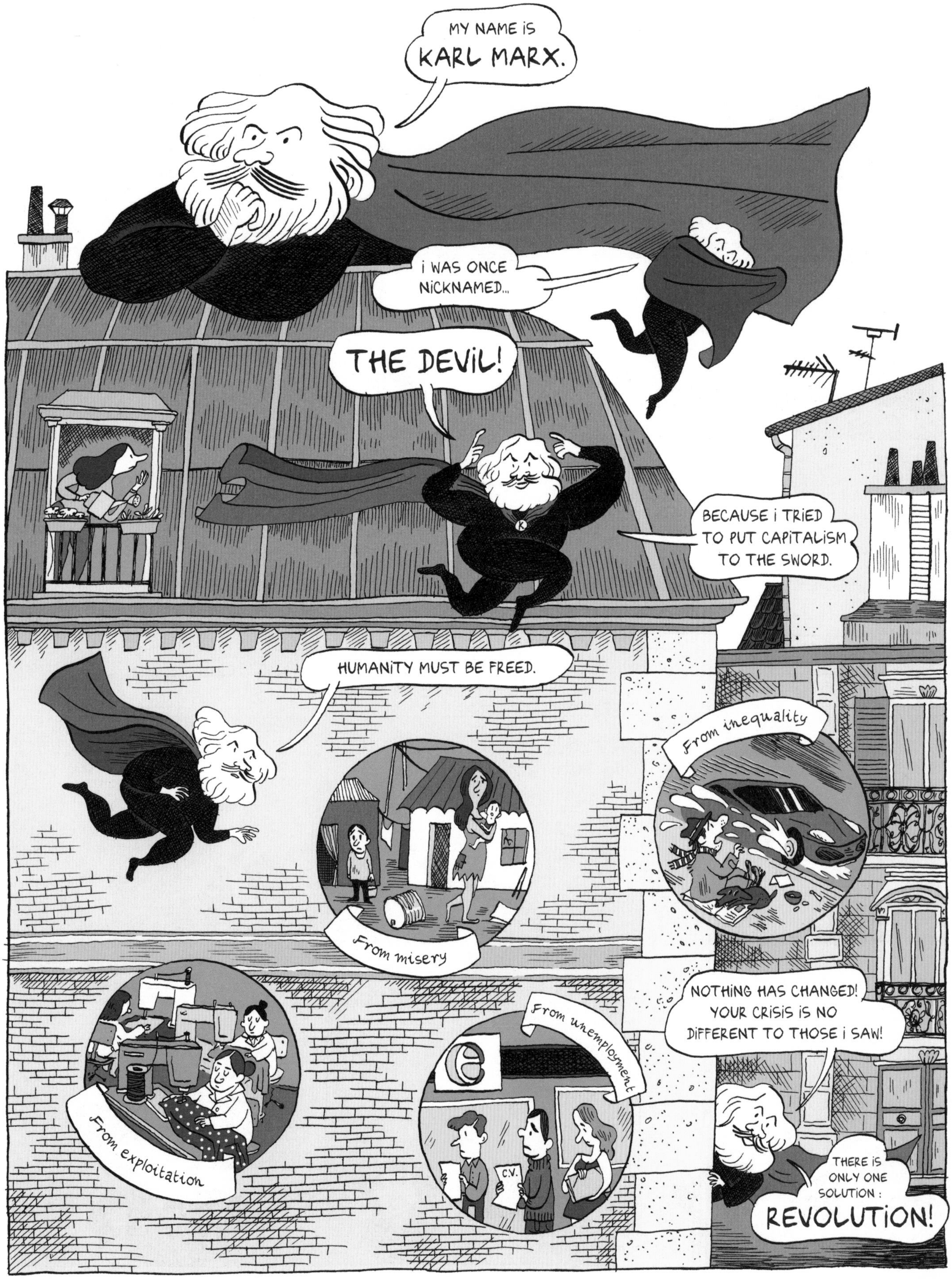

MY NAME IS
KARL MARX.
I WAS ONCE NICKNAMED...
THE DEVIL!
BECAUSE I TRIED TO PUT CAPITALISM TO THE SWORD.
HUMANITY MUST BE FREED.
From misery
From inequality
From exploitation
From unemployment
C.V.
NOTHING HAS CHANGED! YOUR CRISIS IS NO DIFFERENT TO THOSE I SAW!
THERE IS ONLY ONE SOLUTION :
REVOLUTION!

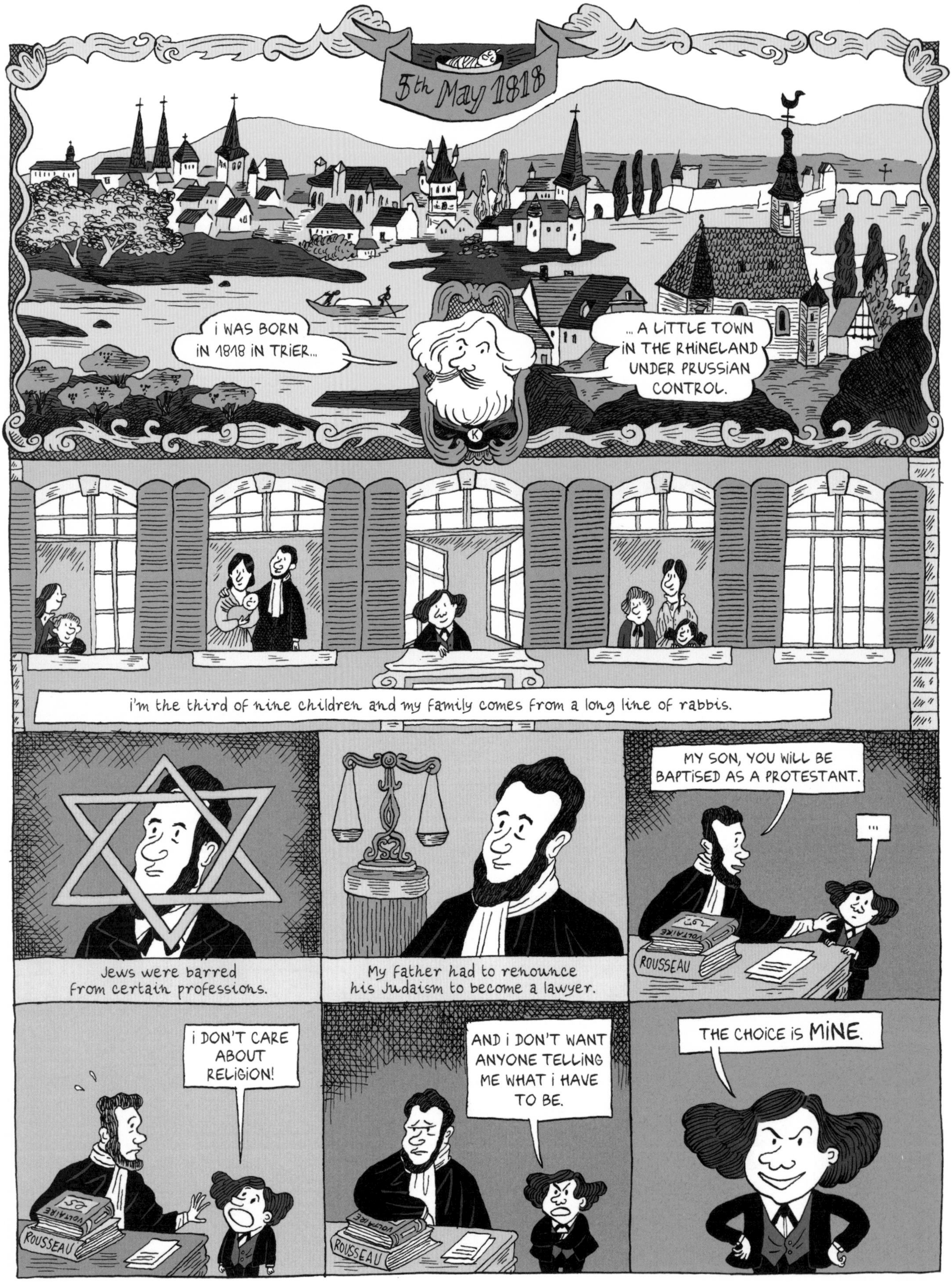
5th May 1818
I WAS BORN IN 1818 IN TRIER...
... A LITTLE TOWN IN THE RHINELAND UNDER PRUSSIAN CONTROL.
I'm the third of nine children and my family comes from a long line of rabbis.
Jews were barred from certain professions.
My father had to renounce his Judaism to become a lawyer.
MY SON, YOU WILL BE BAPTISED AS A PROTESTANT.
...
ROUSSEAU
VOLTAIRE
I DON'T CARE ABOUT RELIGION!
AND I DON'T WANT ANYONE TELLING ME WHAT I HAVE TO BE.
THE CHOICE IS MINE.

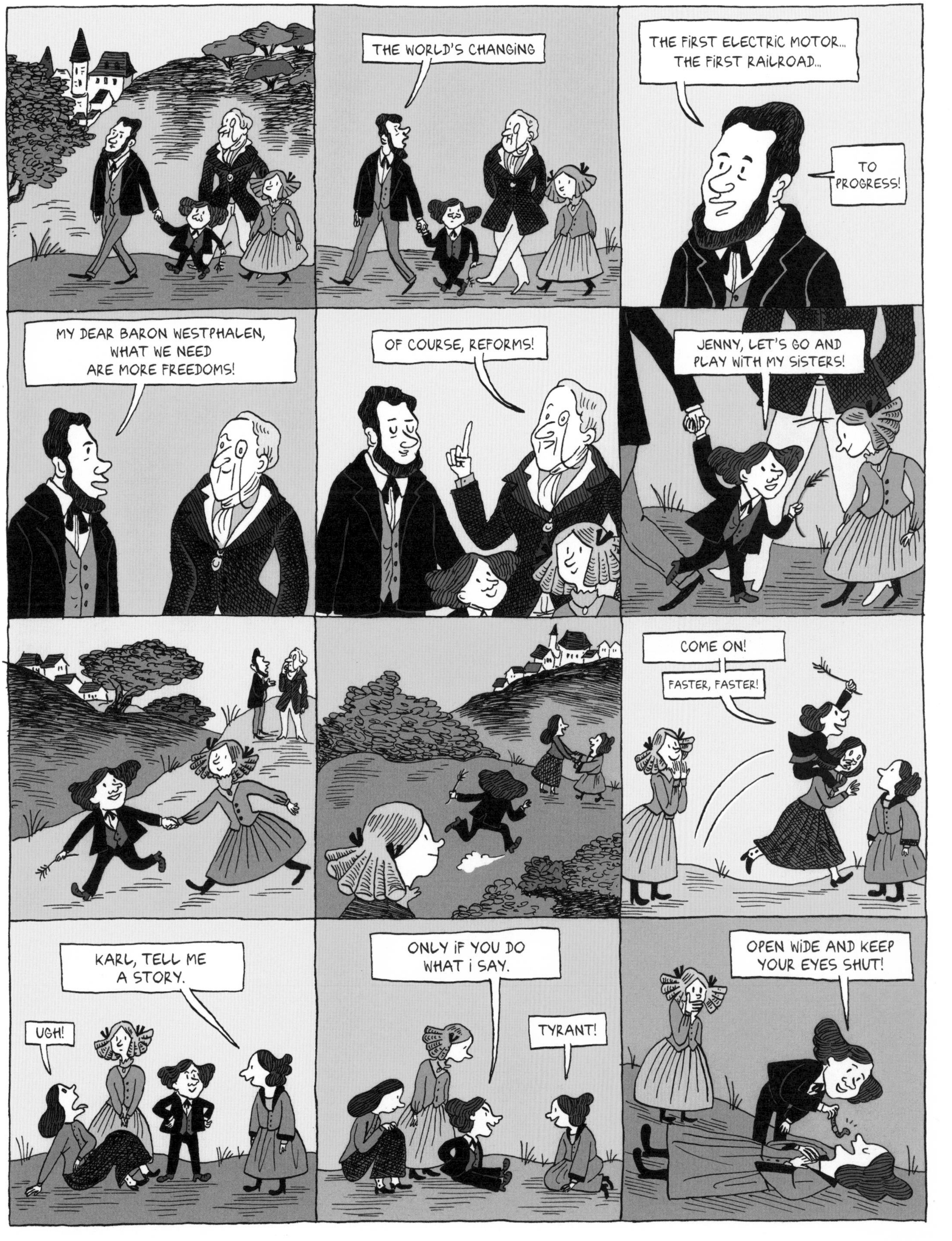
THE WORLD'S CHANGING
THE FIRST ELECTRIC MOTOR... THE FIRST RAILROAD...
TO PROGRESS!
MY DEAR BARON WESTPHALEN, WHAT WE NEED ARE MORE FREEDOMS!
OF COURSE, REFORMS!
JENNY, LET'S GO AND PLAY WITH MY SISTERS!
COME ON!
FASTER, FASTER!
KARL, TELL ME A STORY.
UGH!
ONLY IF YOU DO WHAT I SAY.
TYRANT!
OPEN WIDE AND KEEP YOUR EYES SHUT!

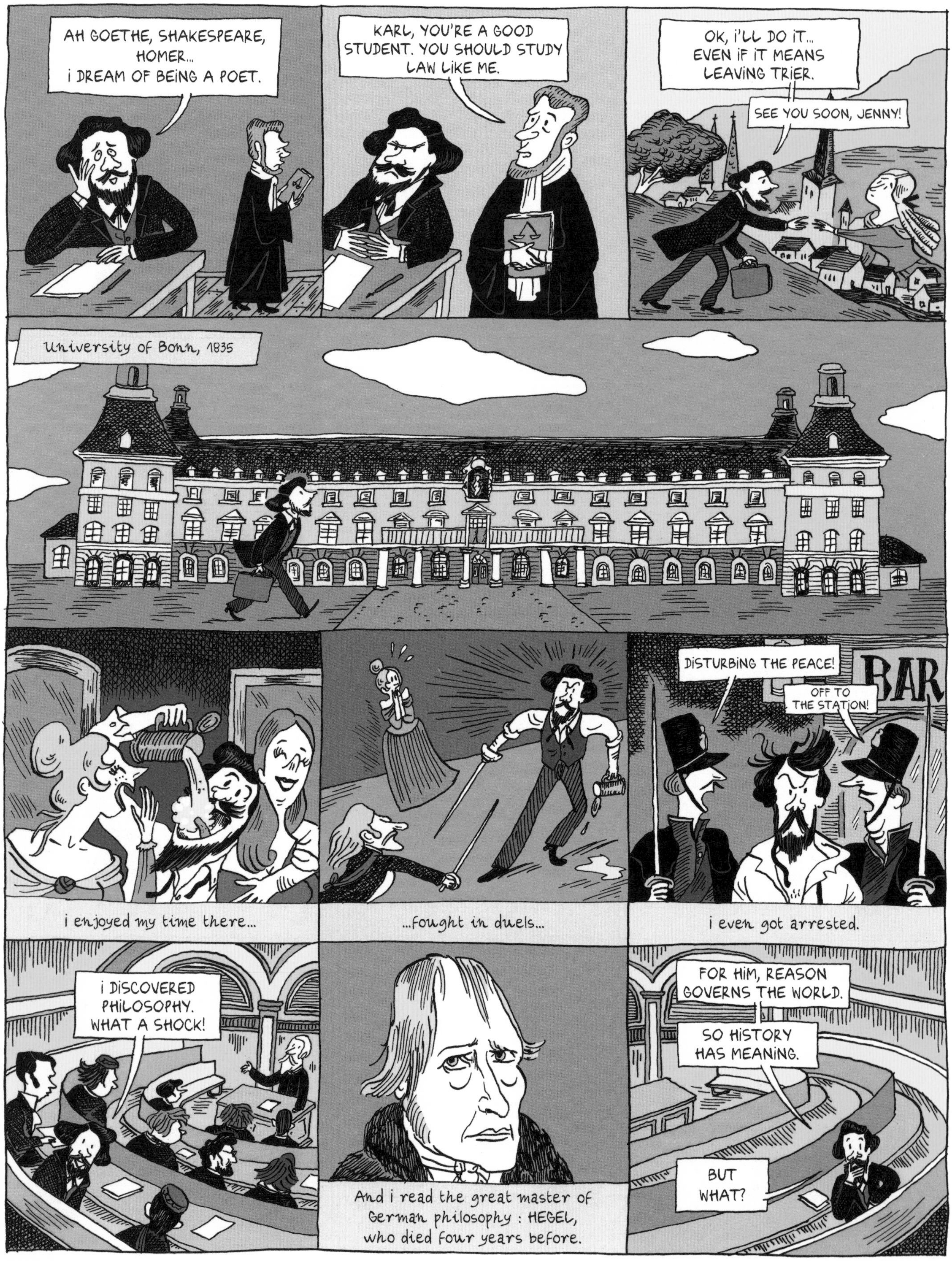
AH GOETHE, SHAKESPEARE, HOMER... I DREAM OF BEING A POET.
KARL, YOU'RE A GOOD STUDENT. YOU SHOULD STUDY LAW LIKE ME.
OK, I'LL DO IT... EVEN IF IT MEANS LEAVING TRIER.
SEE YOU SOON, JENNY!
University of Bonn, 1835
I enjoyed my time there...
...fought in duels...
DISTURBING THE PEACE!
OFF TO THE STATION!
BAR
I even got arrested.
I DISCOVERED PHILOSOPHY. WHAT A SHOCK!
And I read the great master of German philosophy : HEGEL, who died four years before.
FOR HIM, REASON GOVERNS THE WORLD.
SO HISTORY HAS MEANING.
BUT WHAT?

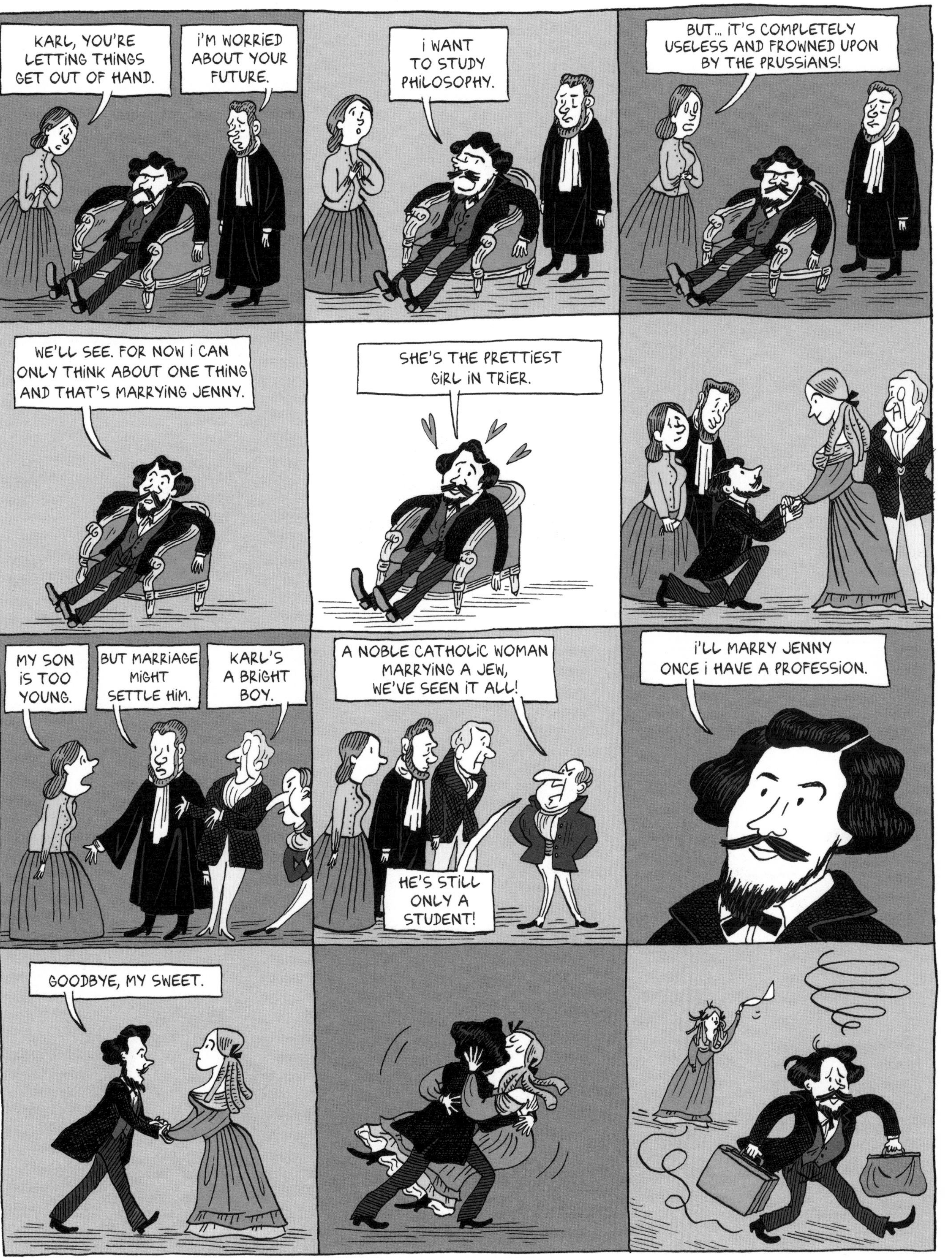
KARL, YOU'RE LETTING THINGS GET OUT OF HAND.
I'M WORRIED ABOUT YOUR FUTURE.
I WANT TO STUDY PHILOSOPHY.
BUT... IT'S COMPLETELY USELESS AND FROWNED UPON BY THE PRUSSIANS!
WE'LL SEE. FOR NOW I CAN ONLY THINK ABOUT ONE THING AND THAT'S MARRYING JENNY.
SHE'S THE PRETTIEST GIRL IN TRIER.
MY SON IS TOO YOUNG.
BUT MARRIAGE MIGHT SETTLE HIM.
KARL'S A BRIGHT BOY.
A NOBLE CATHOLIC WOMAN MARRYING A JEW, WE'VE SEEN IT ALL!
HE'S STILL ONLY A STUDENT!
I'LL MARRY JENNY ONCE I HAVE A PROFESSION.
GOODBYE, MY SWEET.

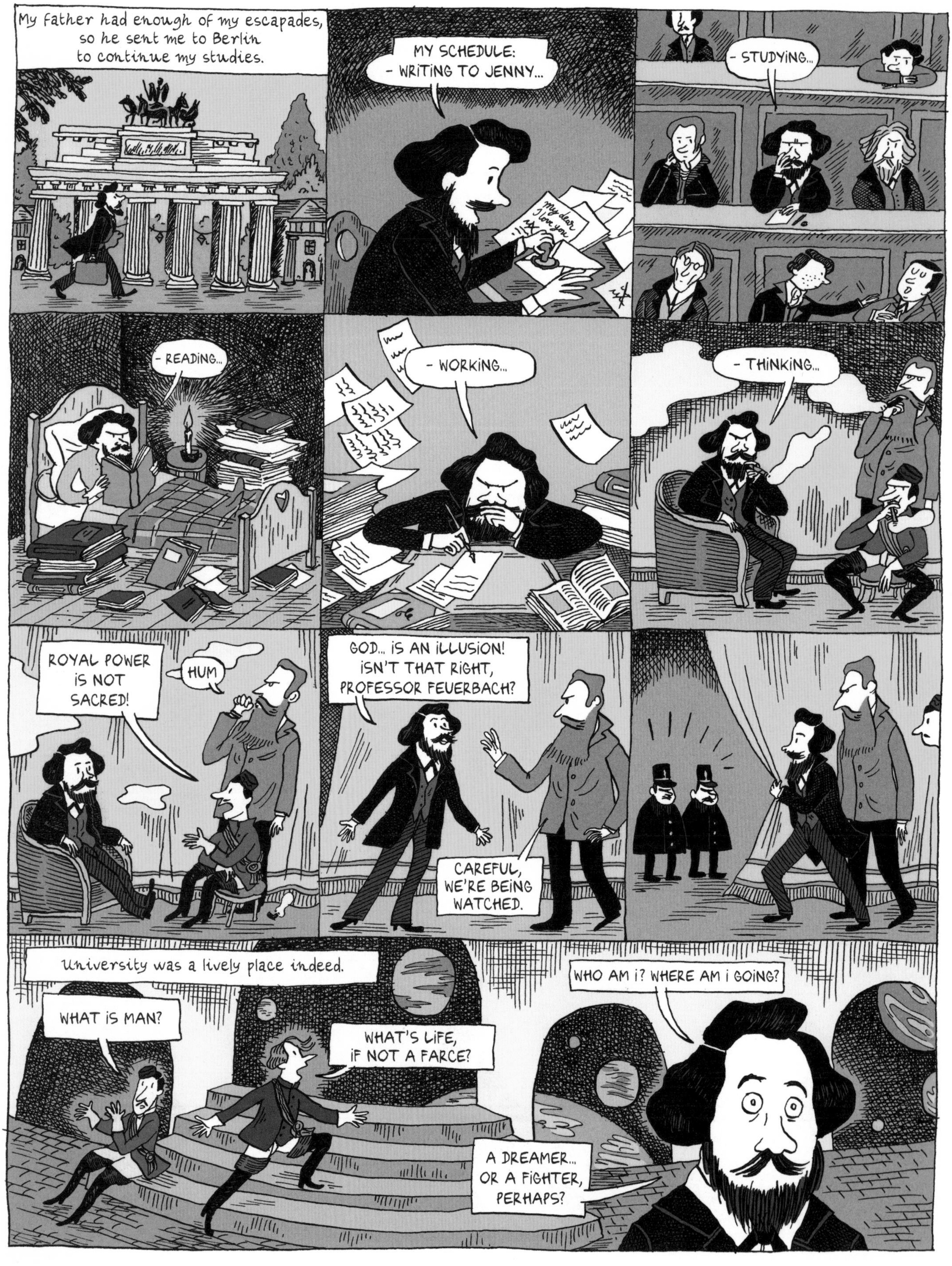
My father had enough of my escapades, so he sent me to Berlin to continue my studies.
MY SCHEDULE: - WRITING TO JENNY...
My dear I love you
- STUDYING...
- READING...
- WORKING...
- THINKING...
ROYAL POWER IS NOT SACRED!
HUM
GOD... IS AN ILLUSION! ISN'T THAT RIGHT, PROFESSOR FEUERBACH?
CAREFUL, WE'RE BEING WATCHED.
University was a lively place indeed.
WHAT IS MAN?
WHAT'S LIFE, IF NOT A FARCE?
WHO AM I? WHERE AM I GOING?
A DREAMER... OR A FIGHTER, PERHAPS?

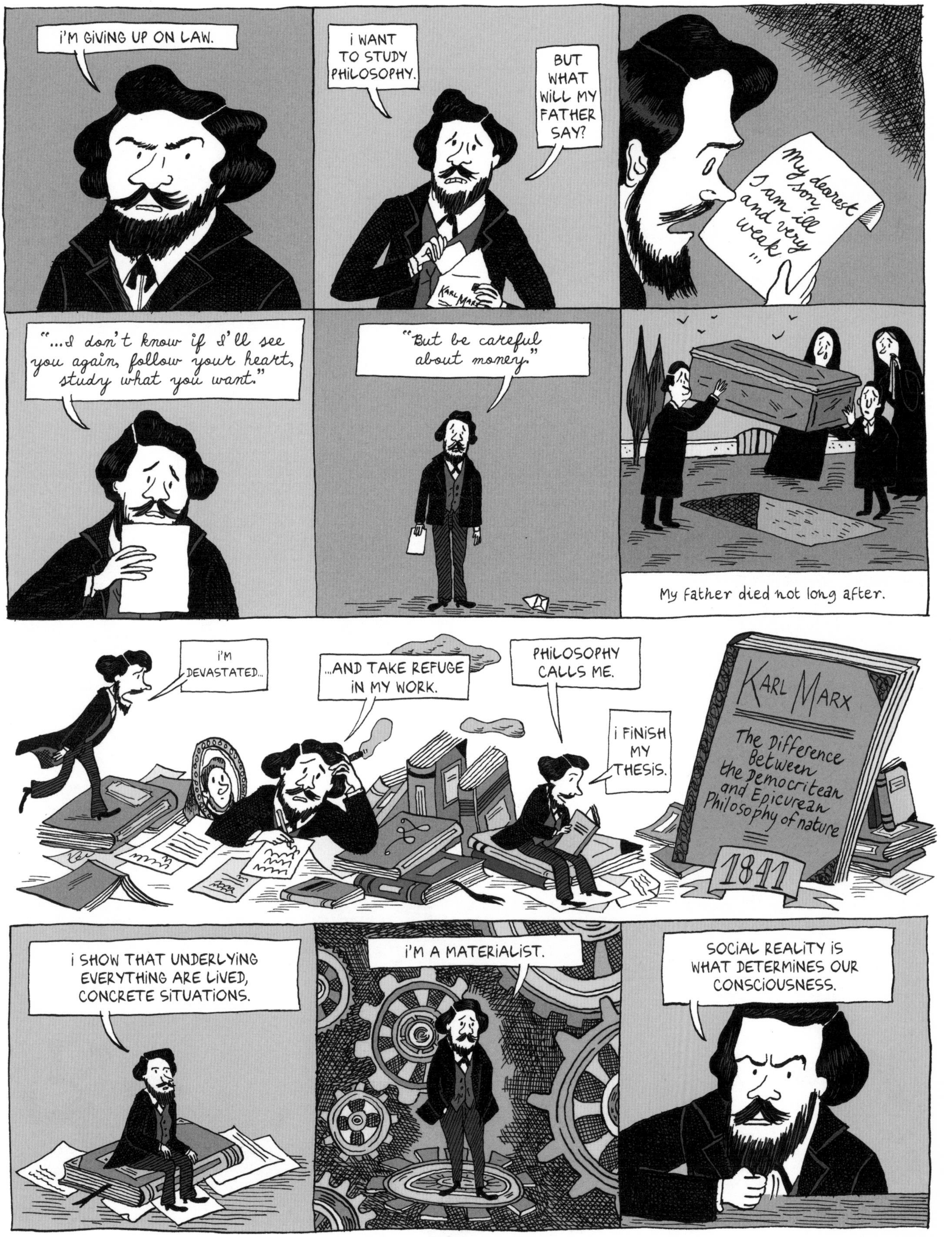
I'M GIVING UP ON LAW.
I WANT TO STUDY PHILOSOPHY.
BUT WHAT WILL MY FATHER SAY?
KARL MARX
My dearest son, I am ill and very weak...
"...I don't know if I'll see you again, follow your heart, study what you want."
"But be careful about money."
My father died not long after.
I'M DEVASTATED...
...AND TAKE REFUGE IN MY WORK.
PHILOSOPHY CALLS ME.
I FINISH MY THESIS.
KARL MARX
The Difference Between the Democritean and Epicurean Philosophy of nature
1841
I SHOW THAT UNDERLYING EVERYTHING ARE LIVED, CONCRETE SITUATIONS.
I'M A MATERIALIST.
SOCIAL REALITY IS WHAT DETERMINES OUR CONSCIOUSNESS.

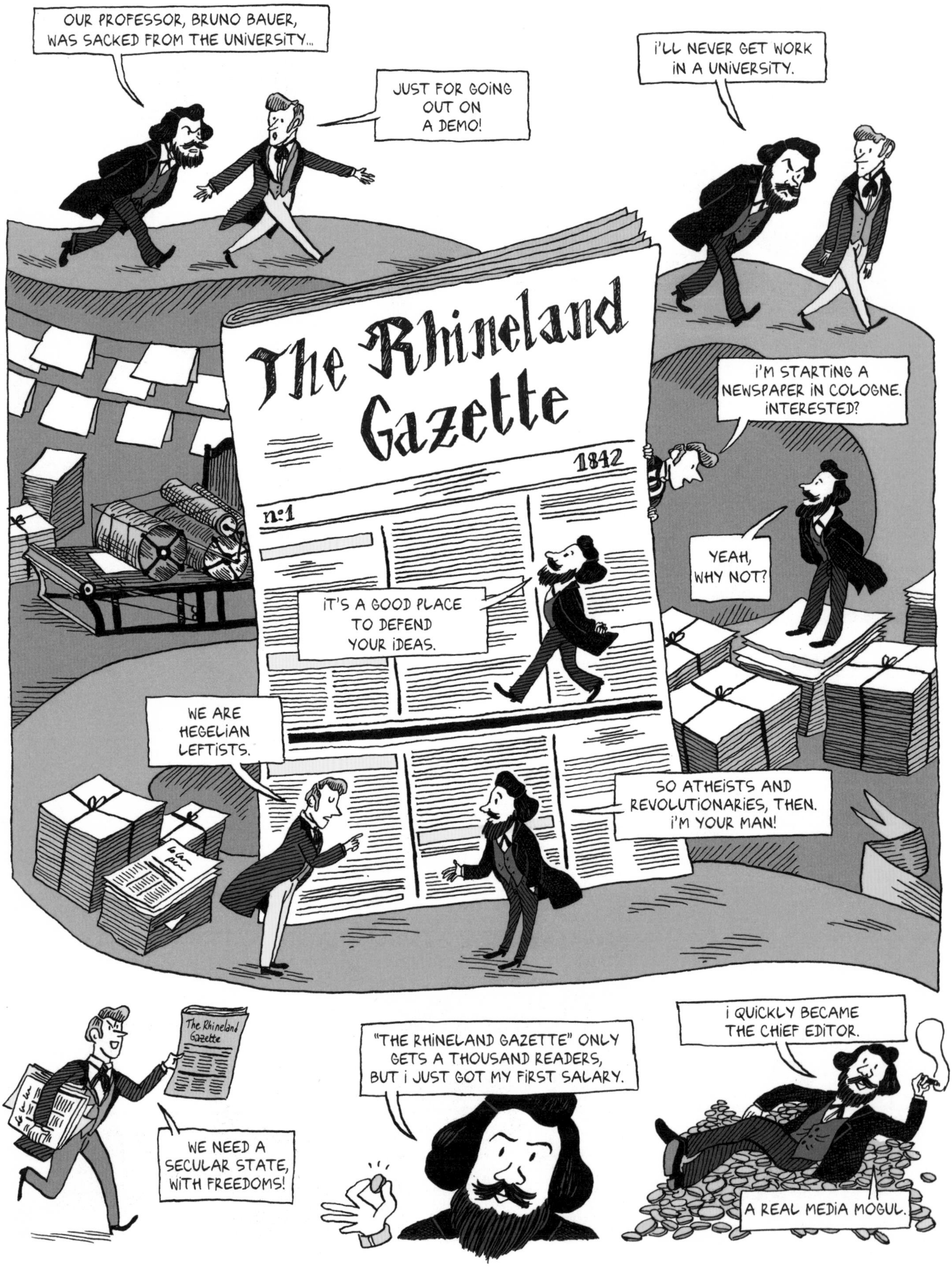
OUR PROFESSOR, BRUNO BAUER, WAS SACKED FROM THE UNIVERSITY...
JUST FOR GOING OUT ON A DEMO!
I'LL NEVER GET WORK IN A UNIVERSITY.
The Rhineland Gazette
1842
nº1
I'M STARTING A NEWSPAPER IN COLOGNE. INTERESTED?
YEAH, WHY NOT?
IT'S A GOOD PLACE TO DEFEND YOUR IDEAS.
WE ARE HEGELIAN LEFTISTS.
SO ATHEISTS AND REVOLUTIONARIES, THEN. I'M YOUR MAN!
The Rhineland Gazette
WE NEED A SECULAR STATE, WITH FREEDOMS!
"THE RHINELAND GAZETTE" ONLY GETS A THOUSAND READERS, BUT I JUST GOT MY FIRST SALARY.
I QUICKLY BECAME THE CHIEF EDITOR.
A REAL MEDIA MOGUL.

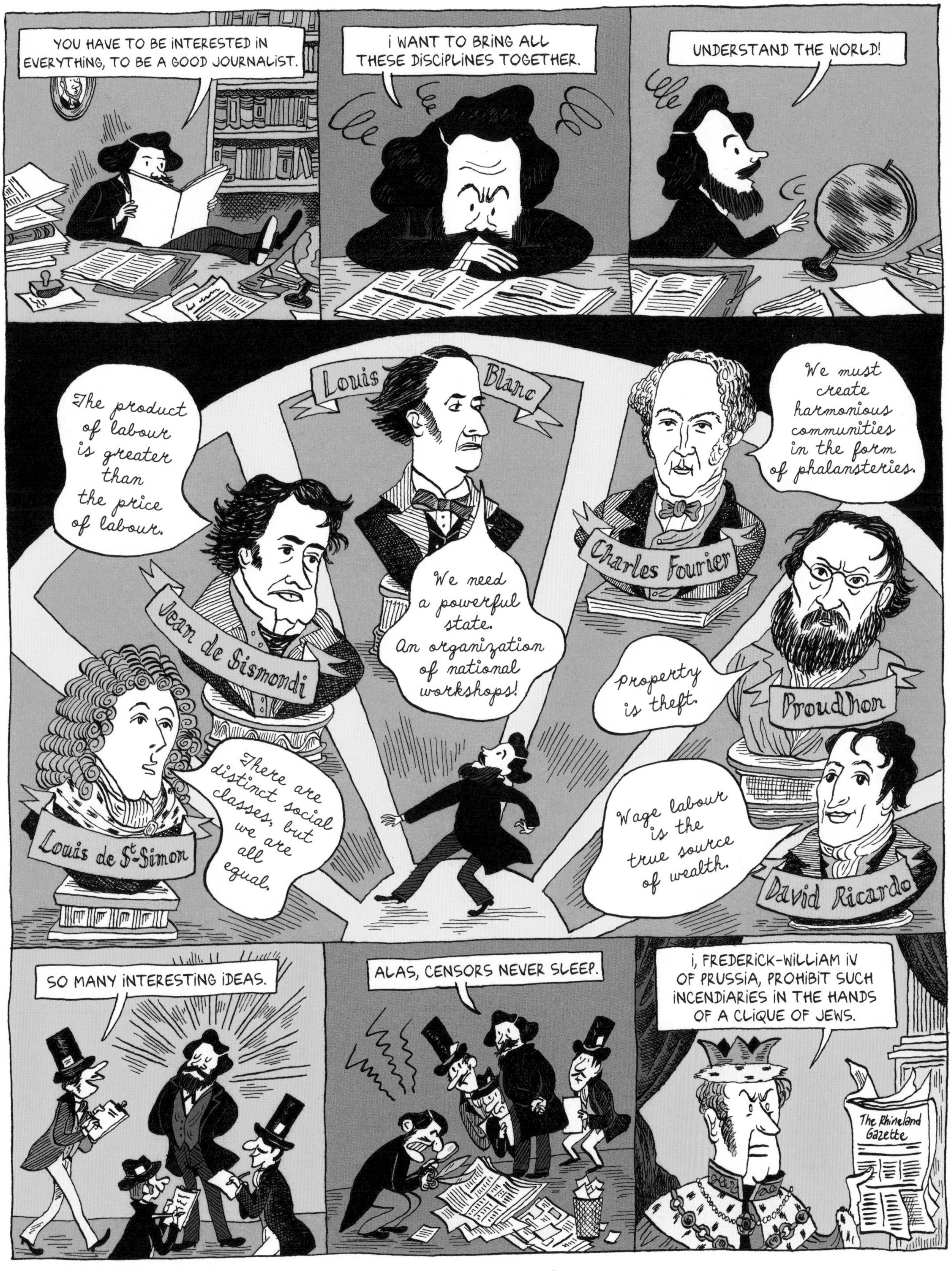

YOU HAVE TO BE INTERESTED IN EVERYTHING, TO BE A GOOD JOURNALIST.
I WANT TO BRING ALL THESE DISCIPLINES TOGETHER.
UNDERSTAND THE WORLD!
Louis Blanc
Charles Fourier
The product of labour is greater than the price of labour.
We must create harmonious communities in the form of phalansteries.
Jean de Sismondi
We need a powerful state. An organization of national workshops!
Proudhon
property is theft.
Louis de St-Simon
There are distinct social classes, but we are all equal.
Wage labour is the true source of wealth.
David Ricardo
SO MANY INTERESTING IDEAS.
ALAS, CENSORS NEVER SLEEP.
I, FREDERICK-WILLIAM IV OF PRUSSIA, PROHIBIT SUCH INCENDIARIES IN THE HANDS OF A CLIQUE OF JEWS.
The Rhineland Gazette

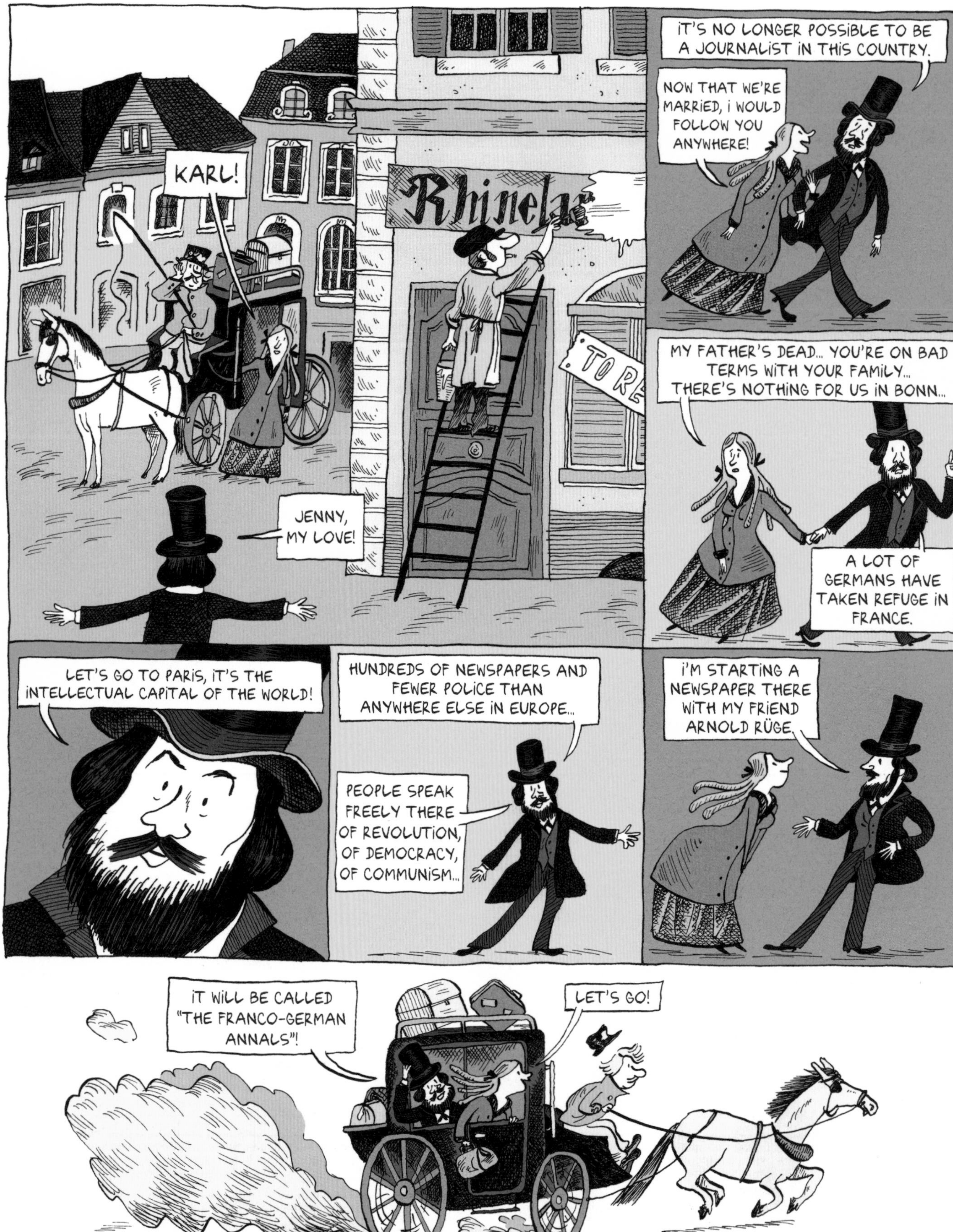
KARL!
JENNY, MY LOVE!
Rhinelar
TO RE
IT'S NO LONGER POSSIBLE TO BE A JOURNALIST IN THIS COUNTRY.
NOW THAT WE'RE MARRIED, I WOULD FOLLOW YOU ANYWHERE!
MY FATHER'S DEAD... YOU'RE ON BAD TERMS WITH YOUR FAMILY... THERE'S NOTHING FOR US IN BONN...
A LOT OF GERMANS HAVE TAKEN REFUGE IN FRANCE.
LET'S GO TO PARIS, IT'S THE INTELLECTUAL CAPITAL OF THE WORLD!
HUNDREDS OF NEWSPAPERS AND FEWER POLICE THAN ANYWHERE ELSE IN EUROPE...
PEOPLE SPEAK FREELY THERE OF REVOLUTION, OF DEMOCRACY, OF COMMUNISM...
I'M STARTING A NEWSPAPER THERE WITH MY FRIEND ARNOLD RÜGE.
IT WILL BE CALLED "THE FRANCO-GERMAN ANNALS"!
LET'S GO!

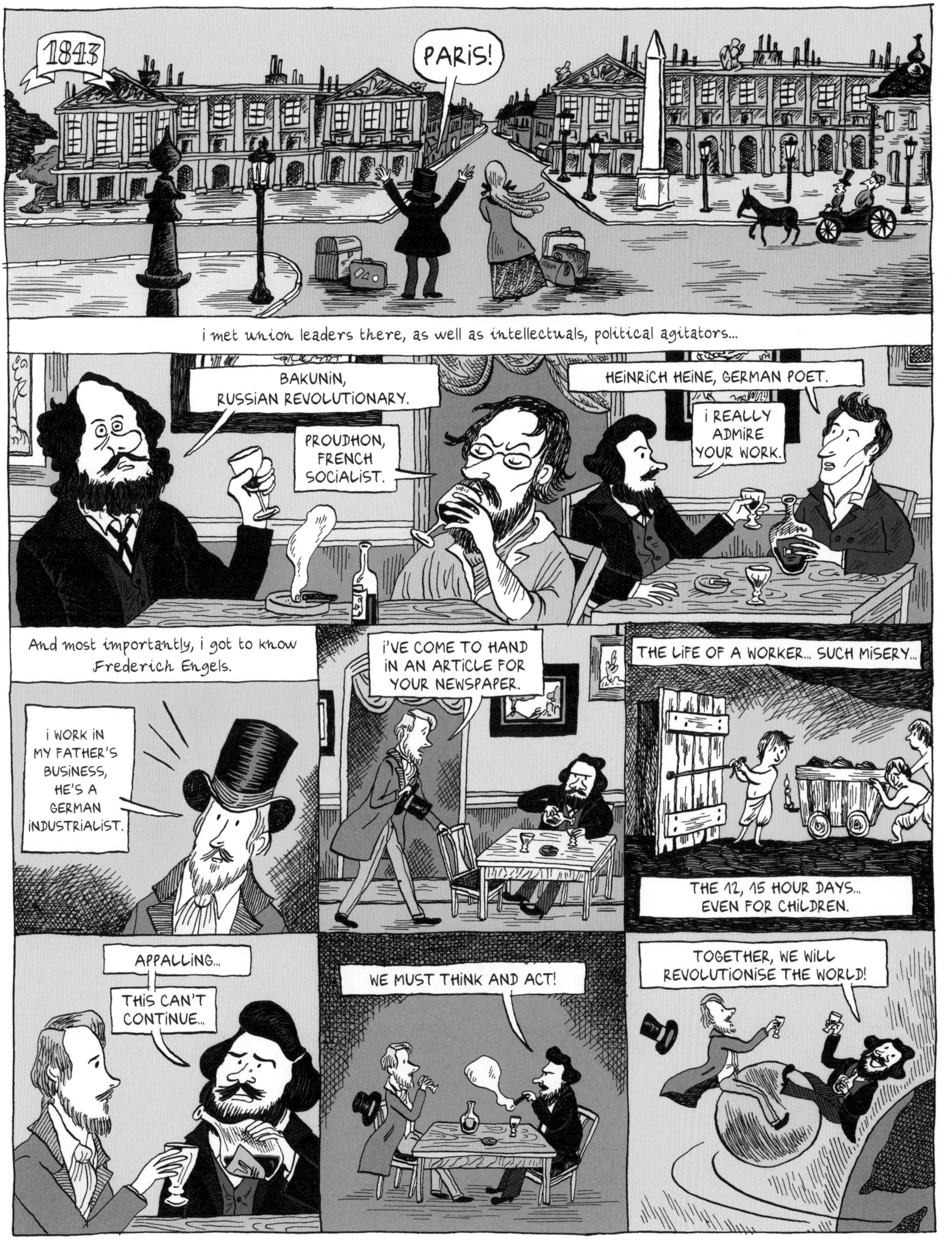
1843
PARiS!
i met union leaders there, as well as intellectuals, political agitators...
BAKUNiN, RUSSiAN REVOLUTiONARY.
PROUDHON, FRENCH SOCiALiST.
HEiNRiCH HEiNE, GERMAN POET.
i REALLY ADMiRE YOUR WORK.
And most importantly, i got to know Frederich Engels.
i WORK iN MY FATHER'S BUSiNESS, HE'S A GERMAN iNDUSTRiALiST.
i'VE COME TO HAND iN AN ARTiCLE FOR YOUR NEWSPAPER.
THE LiFE OF A WORKER... SUCH MiSERY...
THE 12, 15 HOUR DAYS... EVEN FOR CHiLDREN.
APPALLiNG...
THiS CAN'T CONTiNUE...
WE MUST THiNK AND ACT!
TOGETHER, WE WiLL REVOLUTiONiSE THE WORLD!

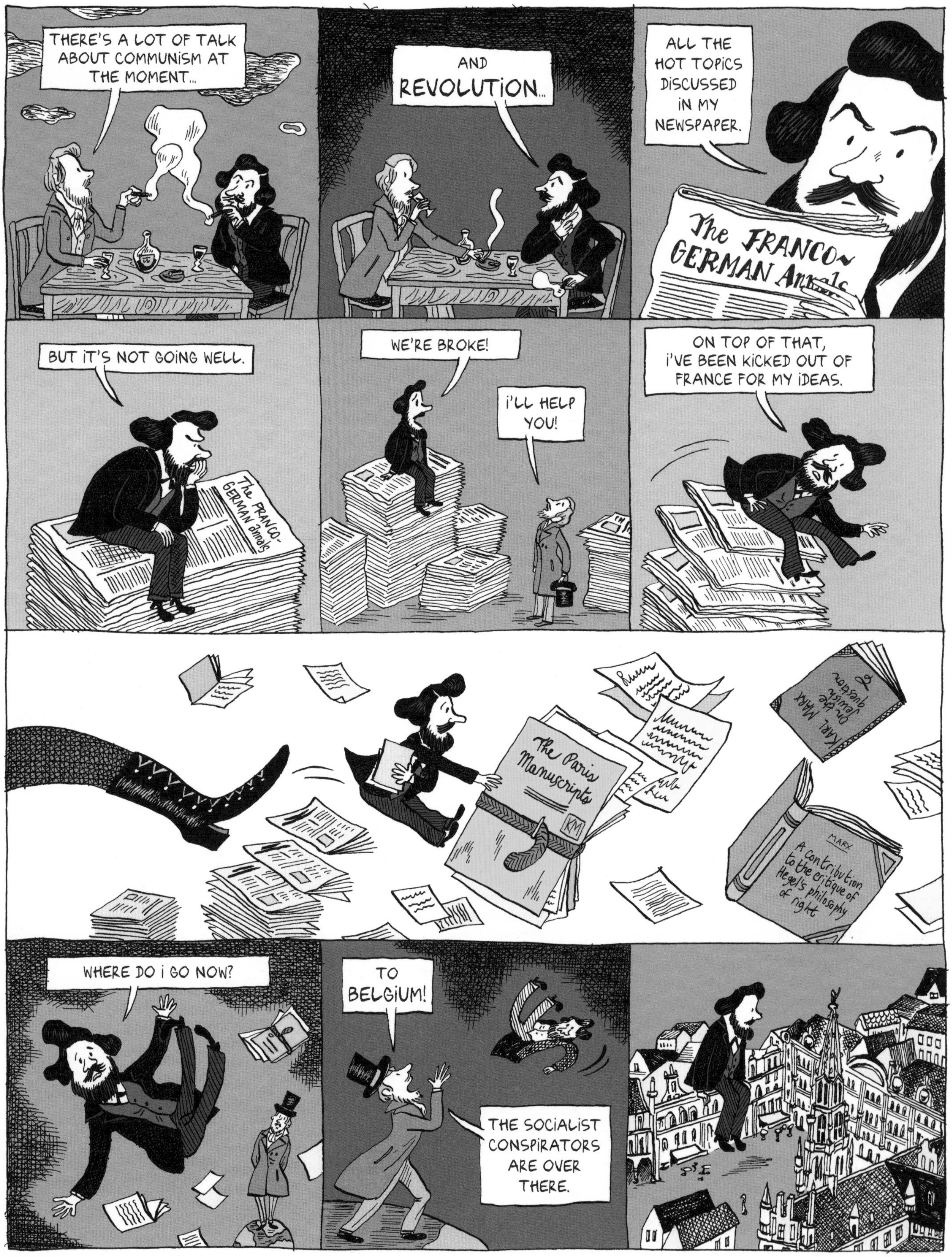
THERE'S A LOT OF TALK ABOUT COMMUNISM AT THE MOMENT...
AND REVOLUTION...
ALL THE HOT TOPICS DISCUSSED IN MY NEWSPAPER.
The FRANCO-GERMAN Annals
BUT IT'S NOT GOING WELL.
The FRANCO-GERMAN annals
WE'RE BROKE!
I'LL HELP YOU!
ON TOP OF THAT, I'VE BEEN KICKED OUT OF FRANCE FOR MY IDEAS.
The Paris Manuscripts
KM
KARL MARX On the Jewish question
MARX A Contribution to the critique of Hegel's philosophy of right
WHERE DO I GO NOW?
TO BELGIUM!
THE SOCIALIST CONSPIRATORS ARE OVER THERE.

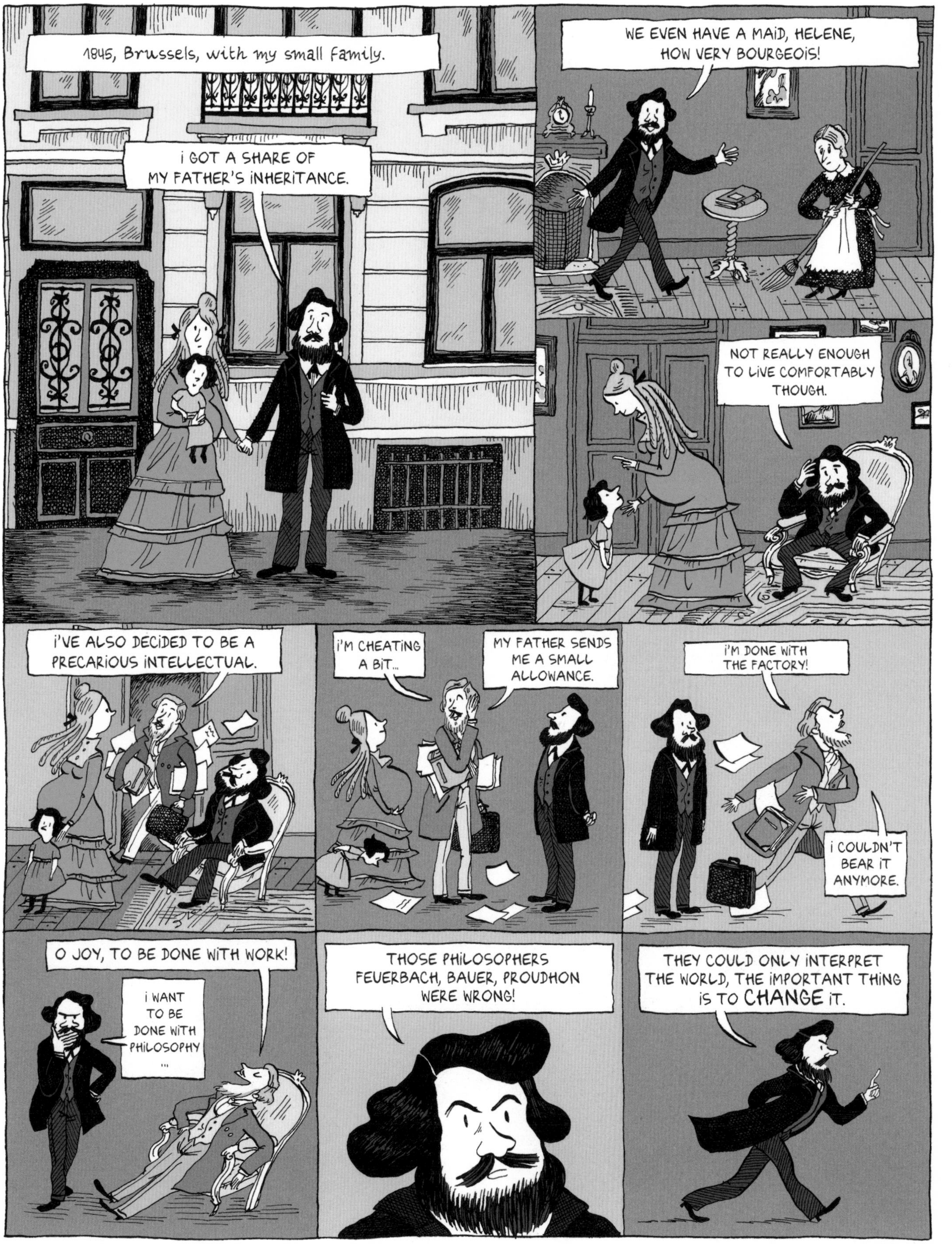
1845, Brussels, with my small family.
I GOT A SHARE OF MY FATHER'S INHERITANCE.
WE EVEN HAVE A MAID, HELENE, HOW VERY BOURGEOIS!
NOT REALLY ENOUGH TO LIVE COMFORTABLY THOUGH.
I'VE ALSO DECIDED TO BE A PRECARIOUS INTELLECTUAL.
I'M CHEATING A BIT...
MY FATHER SENDS ME A SMALL ALLOWANCE.
I'M DONE WITH THE FACTORY!
I COULDN'T BEAR IT ANYMORE.
O JOY, TO BE DONE WITH WORK!
I WANT TO BE DONE WITH PHILOSOPHY ...
THOSE PHILOSOPHERS FEUERBACH, BAUER, PROUDHON WERE WRONG!
THEY COULD ONLY INTERPRET THE WORLD, THE IMPORTANT THING IS TO CHANGE IT.

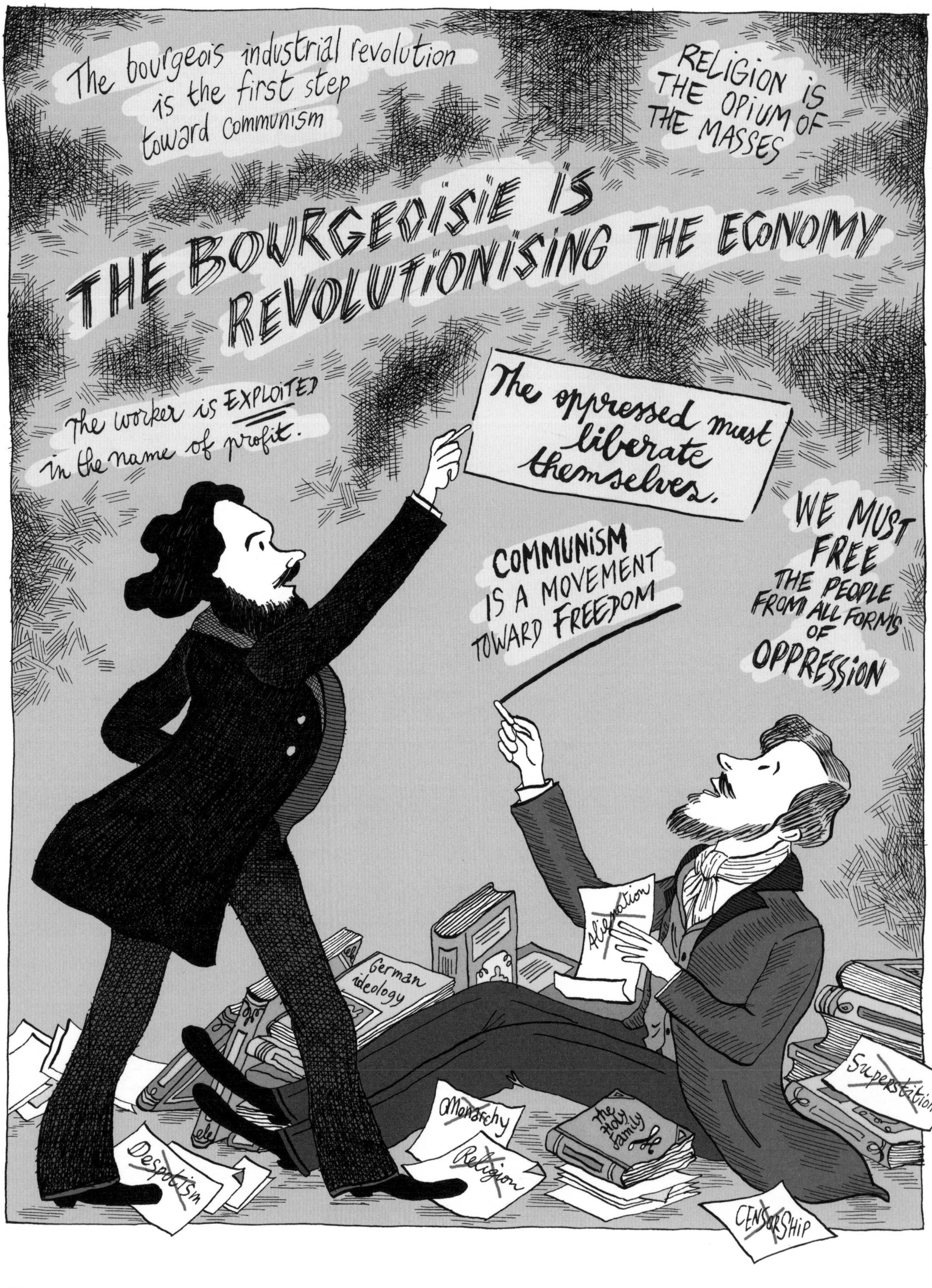
The bourgeois industrial revolution is the first step toward communism
RELIGION IS THE OPIUM OF THE MASSES
THE BOURGEOISIE IS REVOLUTIONISING THE ECONOMY
The worker is EXPLOITED in the name of profit.
The oppressed must liberate themselves.
COMMUNISM IS A MOVEMENT TOWARD FREEDOM
WE MUST FREE THE PEOPLE FROM ALL FORMS OF OPPRESSION
Alienation
German ideology
Superstitions
Monarchy
The Holy Family
Despotism
Religion
CENSORSHIP

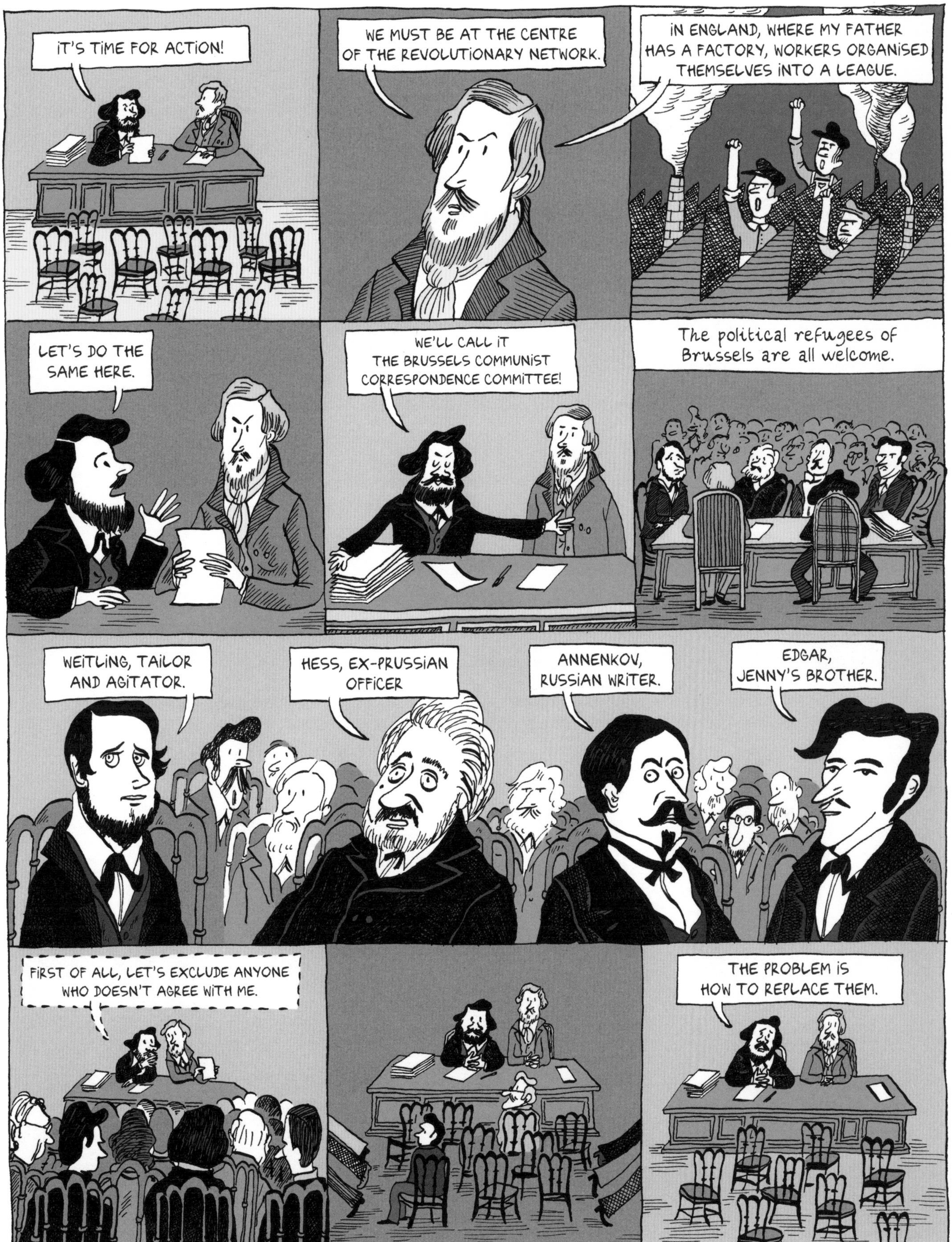
IT'S TIME FOR ACTION!
WE MUST BE AT THE CENTRE OF THE REVOLUTIONARY NETWORK.
IN ENGLAND, WHERE MY FATHER HAS A FACTORY, WORKERS ORGANISED THEMSELVES INTO A LEAGUE.
LET'S DO THE SAME HERE.
WE'LL CALL IT THE BRUSSELS COMMUNIST CORRESPONDENCE COMMITTEE!
The political refugees of Brussels are all welcome.
WEITLING, TAILOR AND AGITATOR.
HESS, EX-PRUSSIAN OFFICER
ANNENKOV, RUSSIAN WRITER.
EDGAR, JENNY'S BROTHER.
FIRST OF ALL, LET'S EXCLUDE ANYONE WHO DOESN'T AGREE WITH ME.
THE PROBLEM IS HOW TO REPLACE THEM.

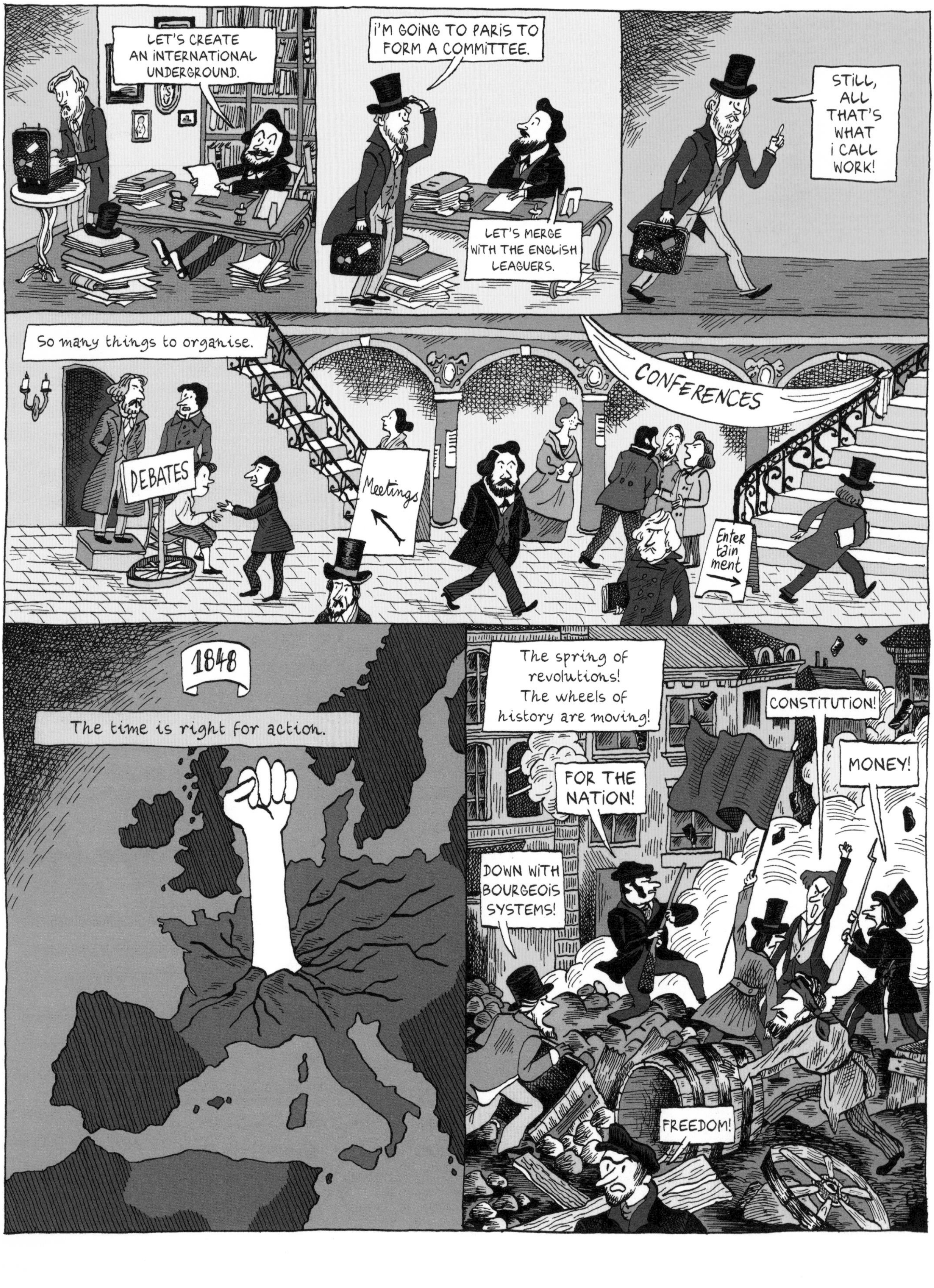
LET'S CREATE AN INTERNATIONAL UNDERGROUND.
I'M GOING TO PARIS TO FORM A COMMITTEE.
LET'S MERGE WITH THE ENGLISH LEAGUERS.
STILL, ALL THAT'S WHAT I CALL WORK!
So many things to organise.
DEBATES
Meetings
CONFERENCES
Enter tain ment
1848
The time is right for action.
The spring of revolutions! The wheels of history are moving!
CONSTITUTION!
MONEY!
FOR THE NATION!
DOWN WITH BOURGEOIS SYSTEMS!
FREEDOM!

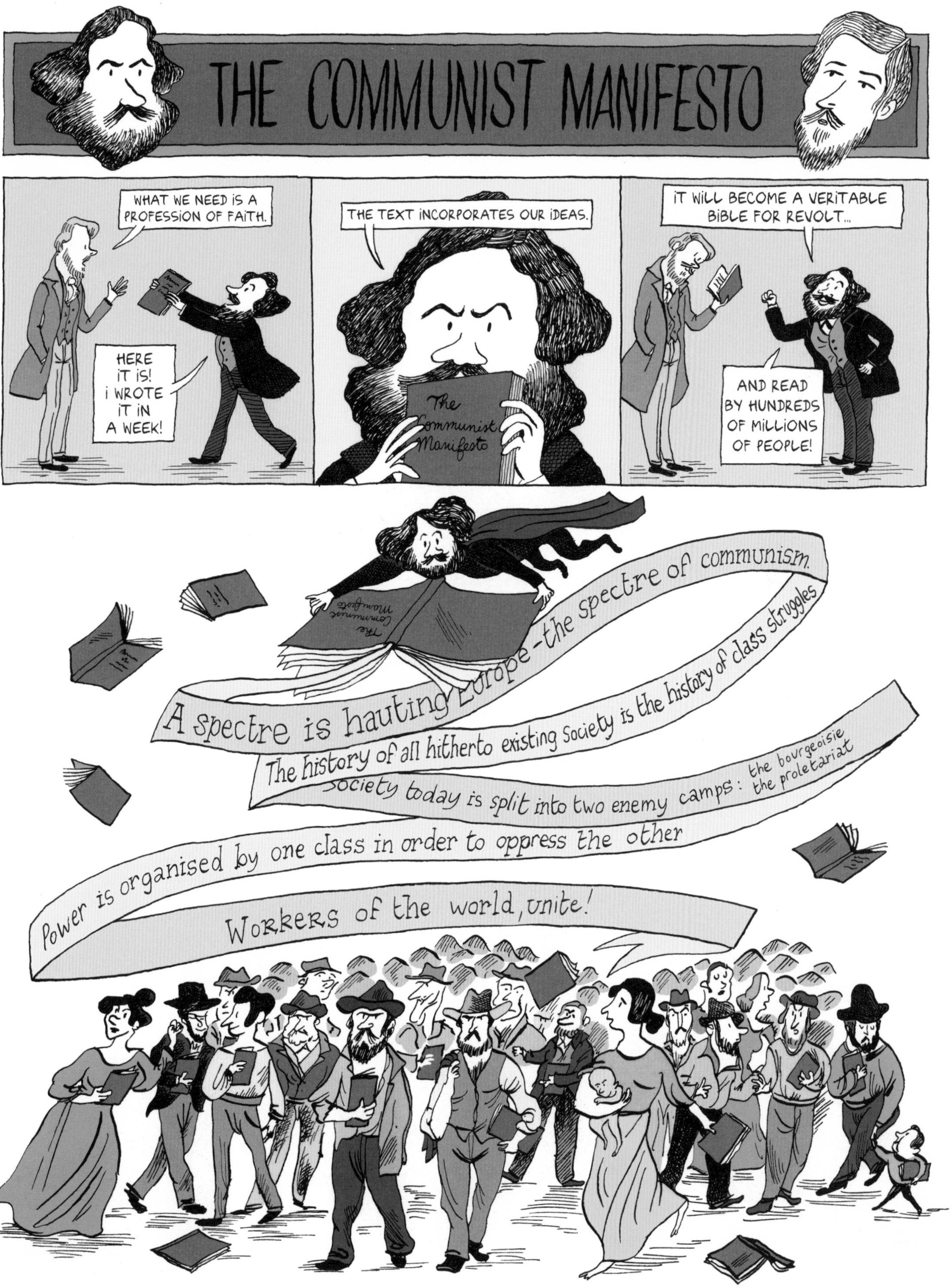
THE COMMUNIST MANIFESTO
WHAT WE NEED IS A PROFESSION OF FAITH.
HERE IT IS! I WROTE IT IN A WEEK!
THE TEXT INCORPORATES OUR IDEAS.
The Communist Manifesto
IT WILL BECOME A VERITABLE BIBLE FOR REVOLT...
AND READ BY HUNDREDS OF MILLIONS OF PEOPLE!
A spectre is hauting Europe - the spectre of communism.
The history of all hitherto existing society is the history of class struggles
Society today is split into two enemy camps: the bourgeoisie the proletariat
Power is organised by one class in order to oppress the other
Workers of the world, unite!

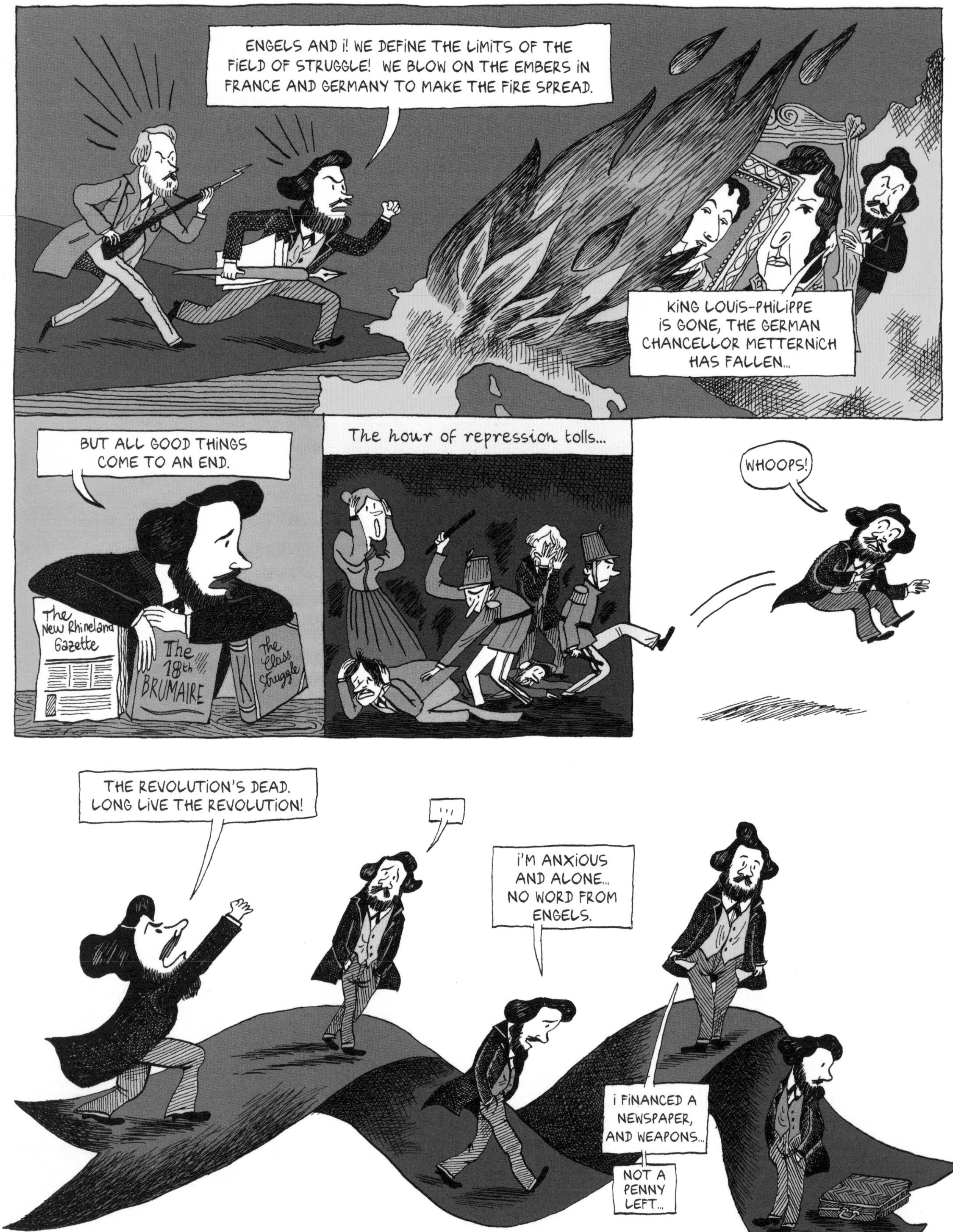
ENGELS AND I! WE DEFINE THE LIMITS OF THE FIELD OF STRUGGLE! WE BLOW ON THE EMBERS IN FRANCE AND GERMANY TO MAKE THE FIRE SPREAD.
KING LOUIS-PHILIPPE IS GONE, THE GERMAN CHANCELLOR METTERNICH HAS FALLEN...
BUT ALL GOOD THINGS COME TO AN END.
The New Rhineland Gazette
The 18th BRUMAIRE
The Class Struggle
The hour of repression tolls...
WHOOPS!
THE REVOLUTION'S DEAD. LONG LIVE THE REVOLUTION!
...
I'M ANXIOUS AND ALONE... NO WORD FROM ENGELS.
I FINANCED A NEWSPAPER, AND WEAPONS...
NOT A PENNY LEFT...

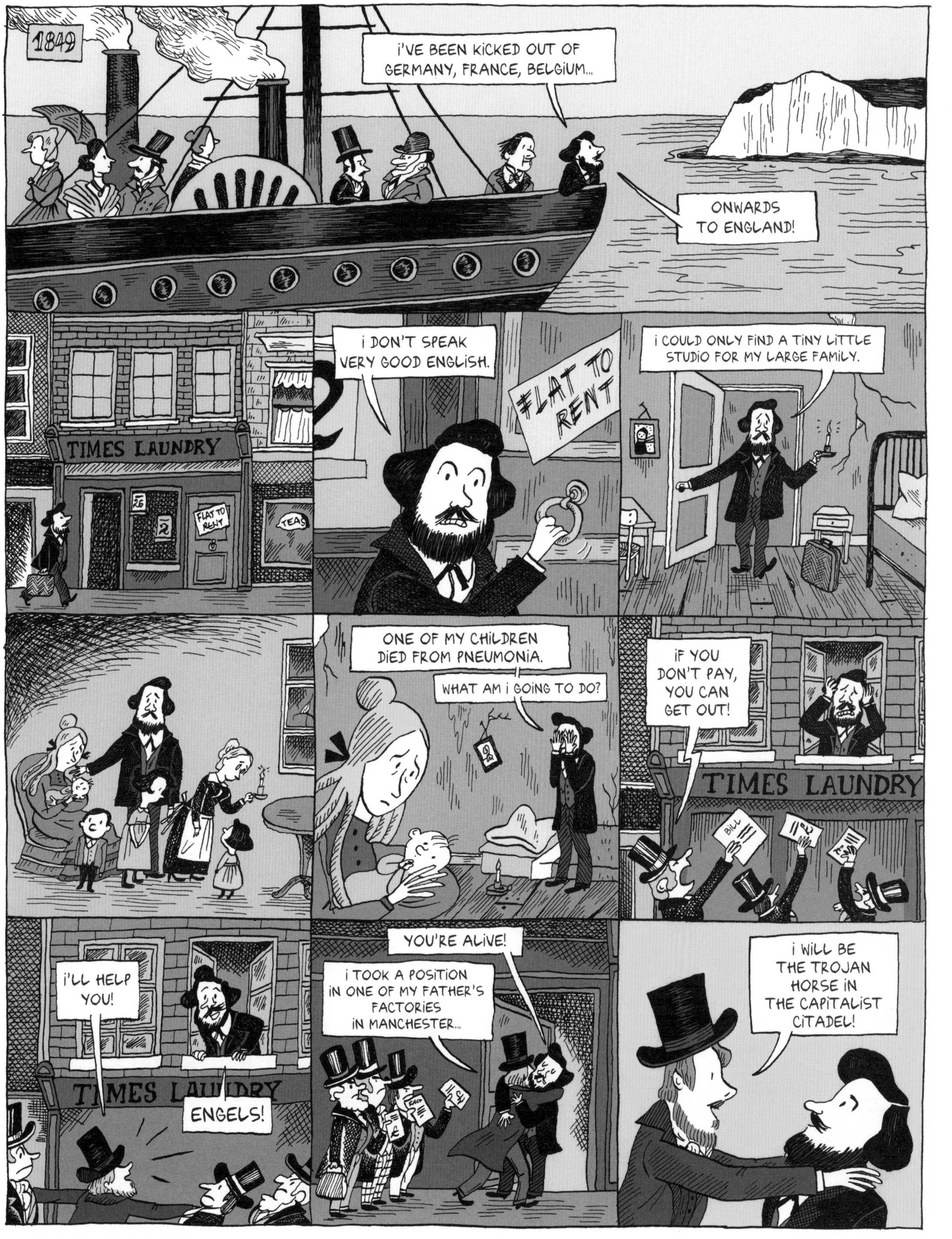
1849
I'VE BEEN KICKED OUT OF GERMANY, FRANCE, BELGIUM...
ONWARDS TO ENGLAND!
TIMES LAUNDRY
FLAT TO RENT
TEAS
I DON'T SPEAK VERY GOOD ENGLISH.
FLAT TO RENT
I COULD ONLY FIND A TINY LITTLE STUDIO FOR MY LARGE FAMILY.
ONE OF MY CHILDREN DIED FROM PNEUMONIA.
WHAT AM I GOING TO DO?
IF YOU DON'T PAY, YOU CAN GET OUT!
TIMES LAUNDRY
BILL
I'LL HELP YOU!
TIMES LAUNDRY
ENGELS!
YOU'RE ALIVE!
I TOOK A POSITION IN ONE OF MY FATHER'S FACTORIES IN MANCHESTER...
I WILL BE THE TROJAN HORSE IN THE CAPITALIST CITADEL!

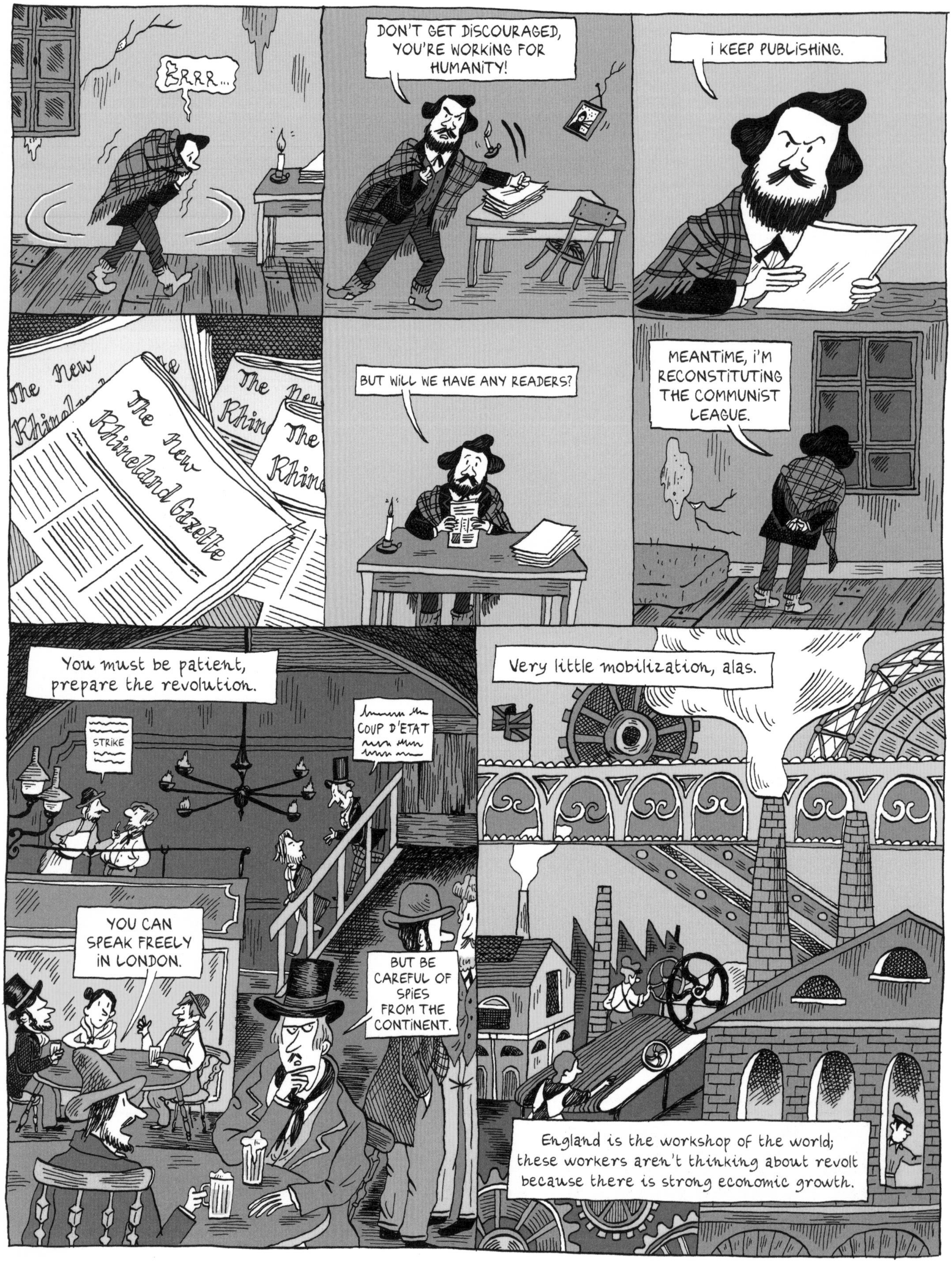
ERRR...
DON'T GET DISCOURAGED, YOU'RE WORKING FOR HUMANITY!
I KEEP PUBLISHING.
The New Rhineland Gazette
BUT WILL WE HAVE ANY READERS?
MEANTIME, I'M RECONSTITUTING THE COMMUNIST LEAGUE.
You must be patient, prepare the revolution.
STRIKE
COUP D'ETAT
YOU CAN SPEAK FREELY IN LONDON.
BUT BE CAREFUL OF SPIES FROM THE CONTINENT.
Very little mobilization, alas.
England is the workshop of the world; these workers aren't thinking about revolt because there is strong economic growth.

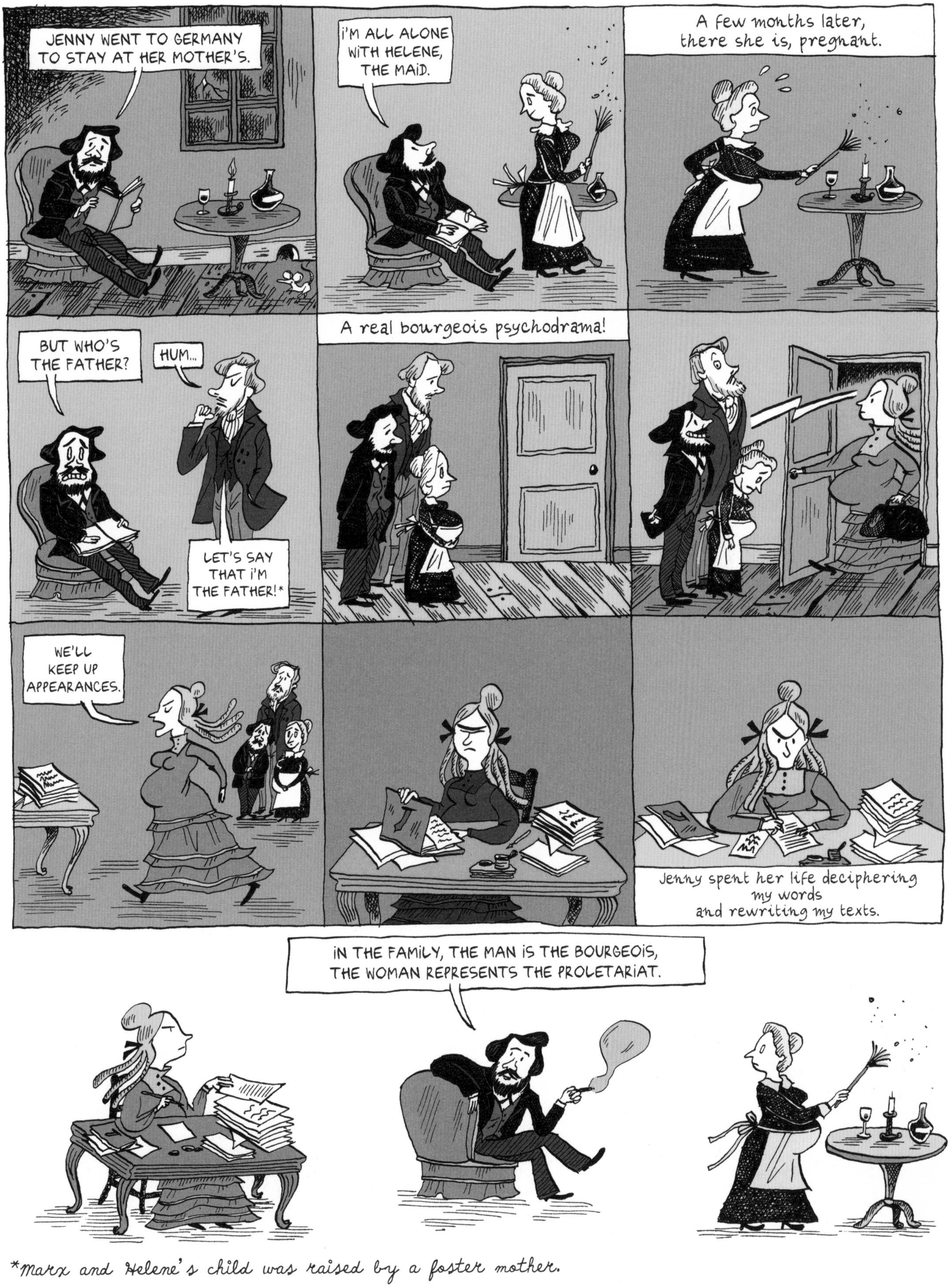
JENNY WENT TO GERMANY TO STAY AT HER MOTHER'S.
I'M ALL ALONE WITH HELENE, THE MAID.
A few months later, there she is, pregnant.
BUT WHO'S THE FATHER?
HUM...
LET'S SAY THAT I'M THE FATHER!*
A real bourgeois psychodrama!
WE'LL KEEP UP APPEARANCES.
Jenny spent her life deciphering my words and rewriting my texts.
IN THE FAMILY, THE MAN IS THE BOURGEOIS, THE WOMAN REPRESENTS THE PROLETARIAT.

*Marx and Helene's child was raised by a foster mother.

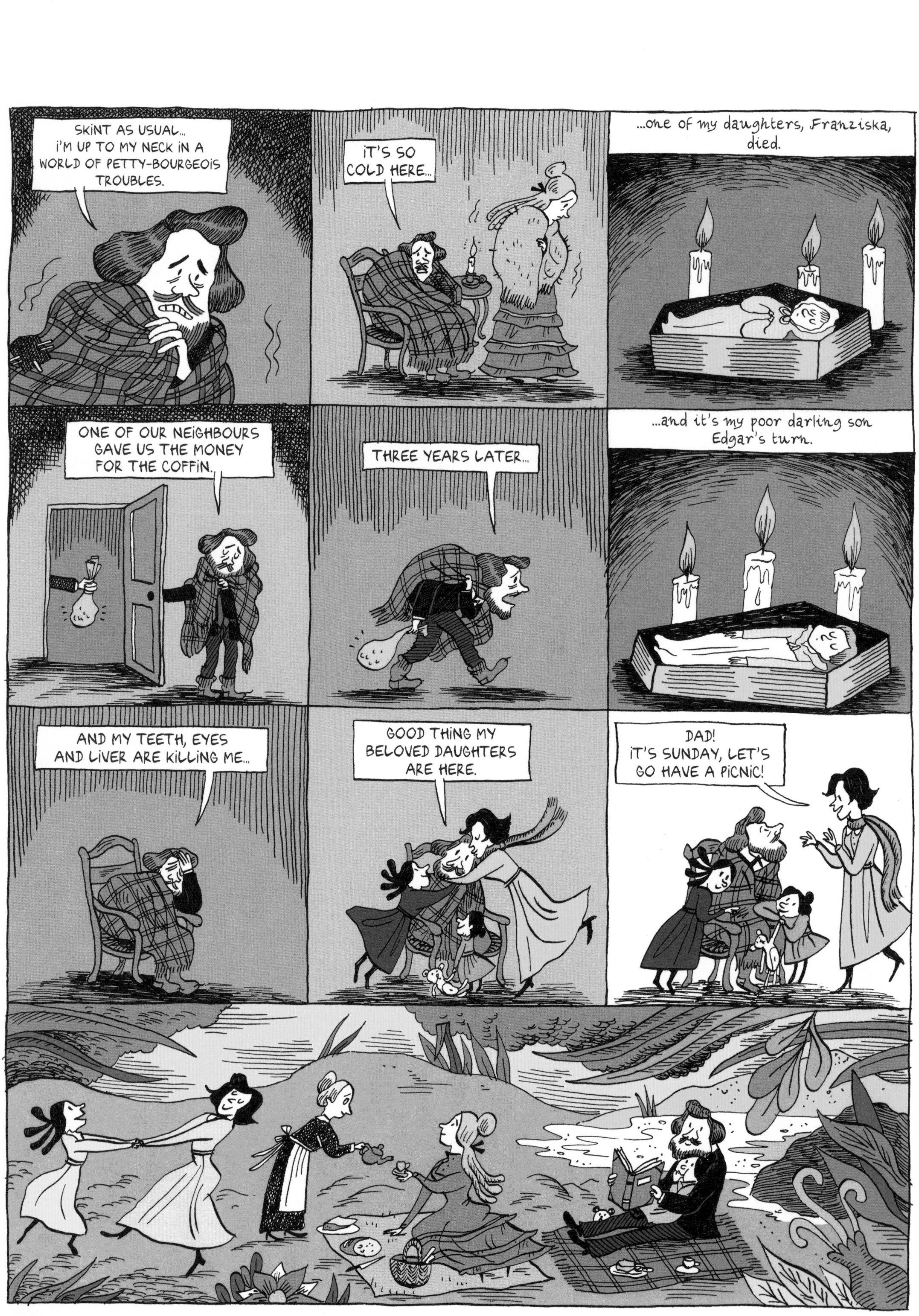
SKINT AS USUAL... I'M UP TO MY NECK IN A WORLD OF PETTY-BOURGEOIS TROUBLES.
IT'S SO COLD HERE...
...one of my daughters, Franziska, died.
ONE OF OUR NEIGHBOURS GAVE US THE MONEY FOR THE COFFIN.
THREE YEARS LATER...
...and it's my poor darling son Edgar's turn.
AND MY TEETH, EYES AND LIVER ARE KILLING ME...
GOOD THING MY BELOVED DAUGHTERS ARE HERE.
DAD! IT'S SUNDAY, LET'S GO HAVE A PICNIC!

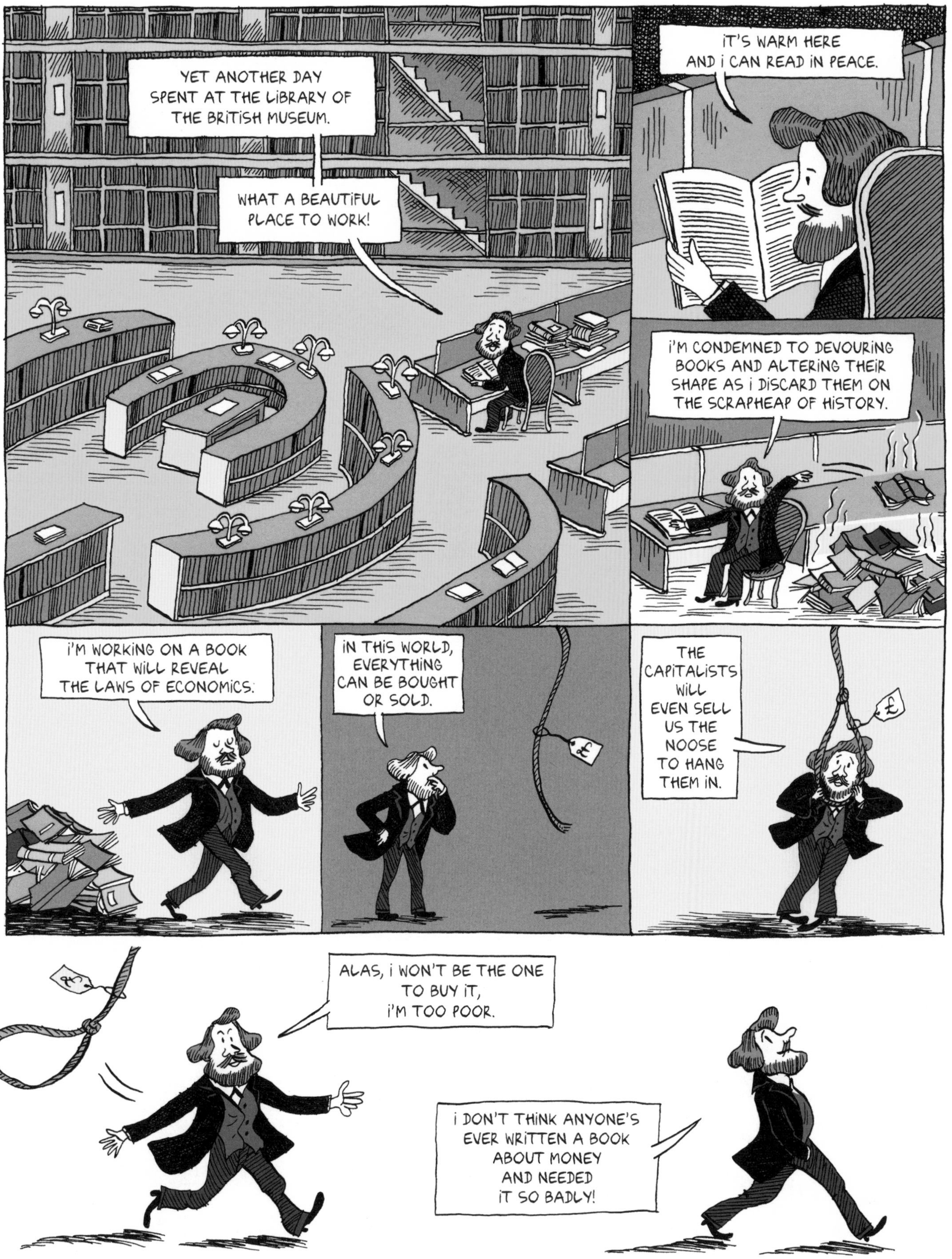
YET ANOTHER DAY SPENT AT THE LIBRARY OF THE BRITISH MUSEUM.
WHAT A BEAUTIFUL PLACE TO WORK!
IT'S WARM HERE AND I CAN READ IN PEACE.
I'M CONDEMNED TO DEVOURING BOOKS AND ALTERING THEIR SHAPE AS I DISCARD THEM ON THE SCRAPHEAP OF HISTORY.
I'M WORKING ON A BOOK THAT WILL REVEAL THE LAWS OF ECONOMICS.
IN THIS WORLD, EVERYTHING CAN BE BOUGHT OR SOLD.
THE CAPITALISTS WILL EVEN SELL US THE NOOSE TO HANG THEM IN.
ALAS, I WON'T BE THE ONE TO BUY IT, I'M TOO POOR.
I DON'T THINK ANYONE'S EVER WRITTEN A BOOK ABOUT MONEY AND NEEDED IT SO BADLY!

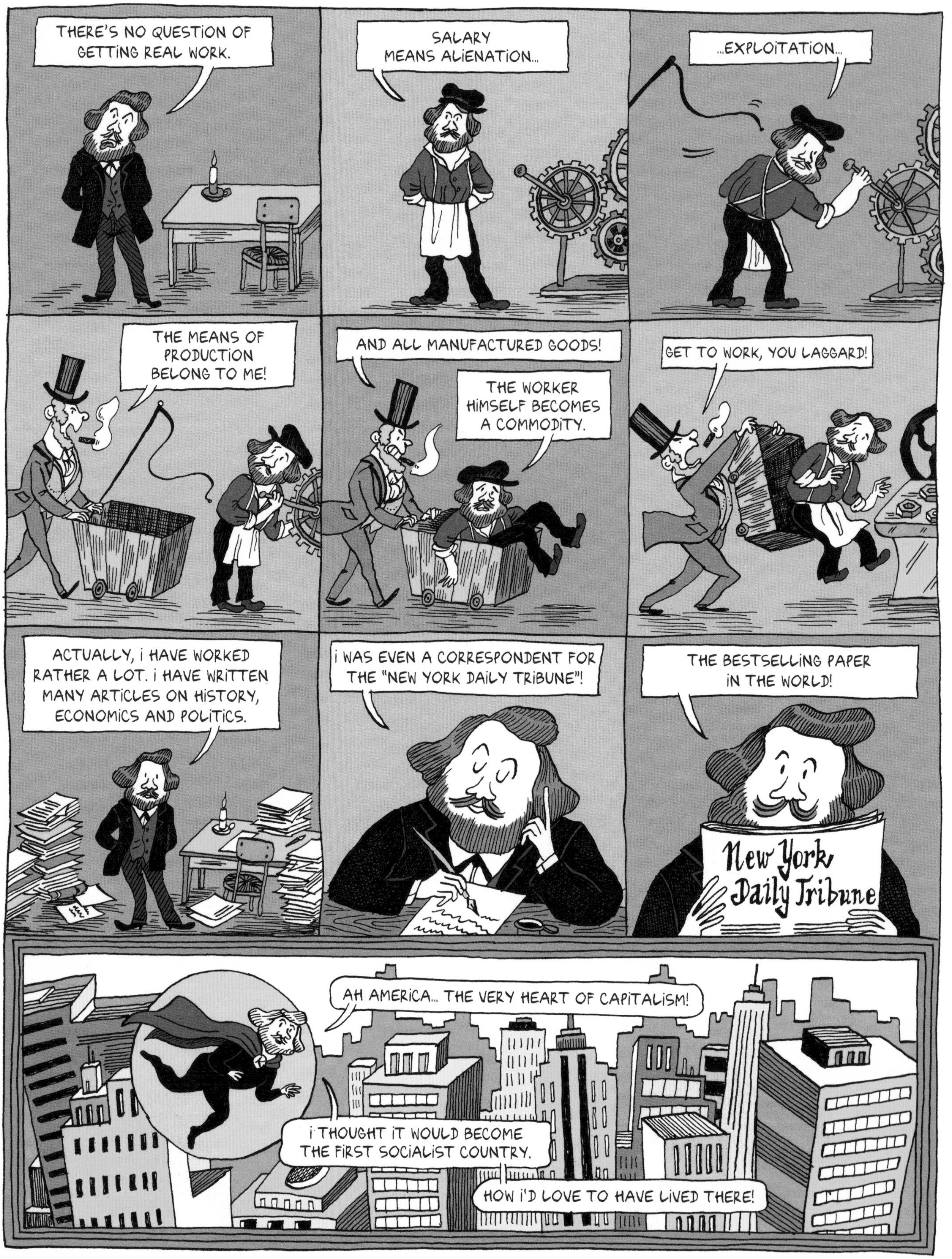
THERE'S NO QUESTION OF GETTING REAL WORK.
SALARY MEANS ALIENATION...
...EXPLOITATION...
THE MEANS OF PRODUCTION BELONG TO ME!
AND ALL MANUFACTURED GOODS!
THE WORKER HIMSELF BECOMES A COMMODITY.
GET TO WORK, YOU LAGGARD!
ACTUALLY, I HAVE WORKED RATHER A LOT. I HAVE WRITTEN MANY ARTICLES ON HISTORY, ECONOMICS AND POLITICS.
I WAS EVEN A CORRESPONDENT FOR THE "NEW YORK DAILY TRIBUNE"!
THE BESTSELLING PAPER IN THE WORLD!
New York Daily Tribune
AH AMERICA... THE VERY HEART OF CAPITALISM!
I THOUGHT IT WOULD BECOME THE FIRST SOCIALIST COUNTRY.
HOW I'D LOVE TO HAVE LIVED THERE!

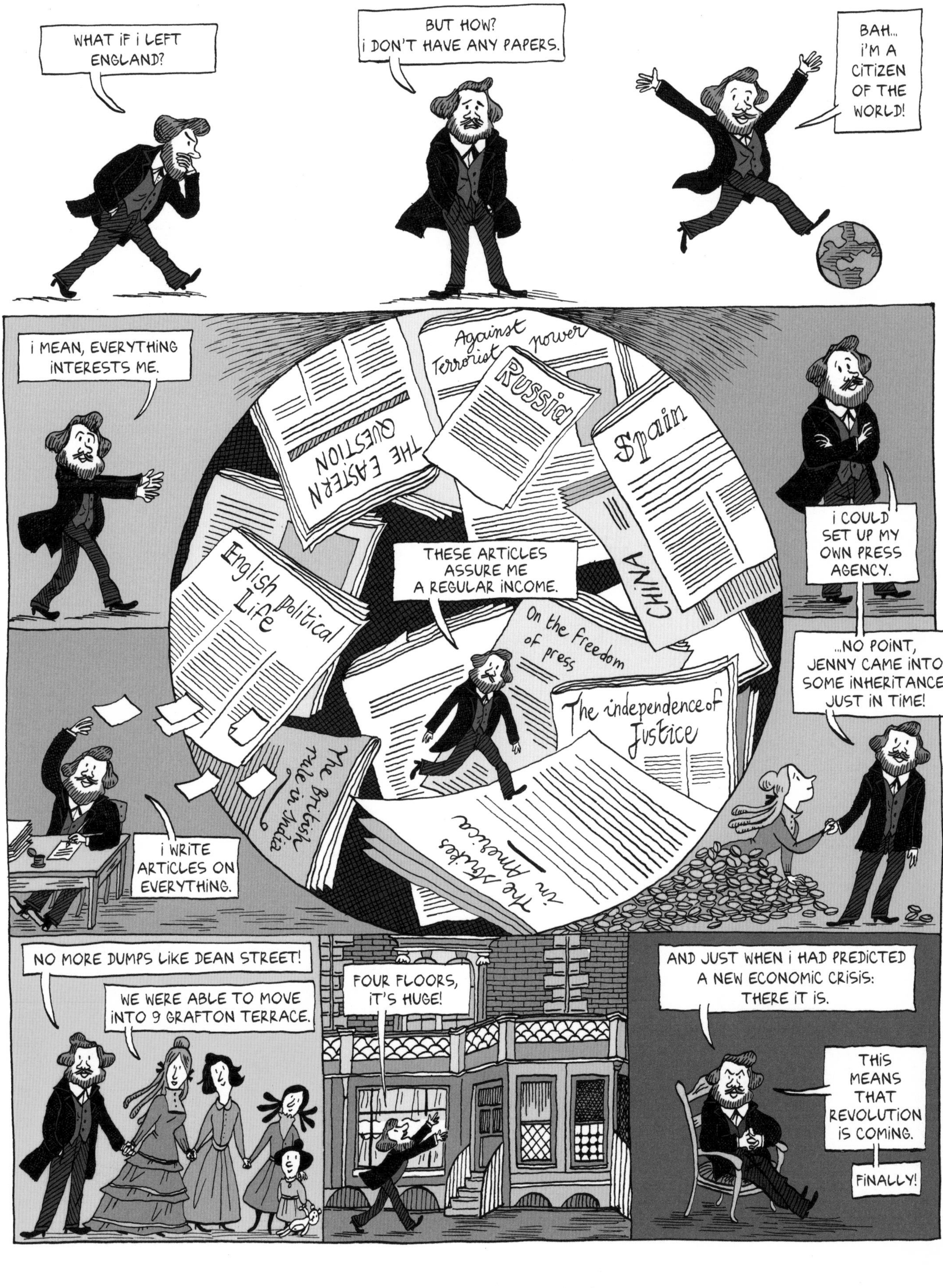
WHAT IF I LEFT ENGLAND?
BUT HOW? I DON'T HAVE ANY PAPERS.
BAH... I'M A CITIZEN OF THE WORLD!
I MEAN, EVERYTHING INTERESTS ME.
Against Terrorist power
Russia
THE EASTERN QUESTION
Spain
CHINA
English political Life
THESE ARTICLES ASSURE ME A REGULAR INCOME.
On the Freedom of press
The independence of Justice
The British rule in India
The Strikes in America
I WRITE ARTICLES ON EVERYTHING.
I COULD SET UP MY OWN PRESS AGENCY.
...NO POINT, JENNY CAME INTO SOME INHERITANCE, JUST IN TIME!
NO MORE DUMPS LIKE DEAN STREET!
WE WERE ABLE TO MOVE INTO 9 GRAFTON TERRACE.
FOUR FLOORS, IT'S HUGE!
AND JUST WHEN I HAD PREDICTED A NEW ECONOMIC CRISIS: THERE IT IS.
THIS MEANS THAT REVOLUTION IS COMING.
FINALLY!

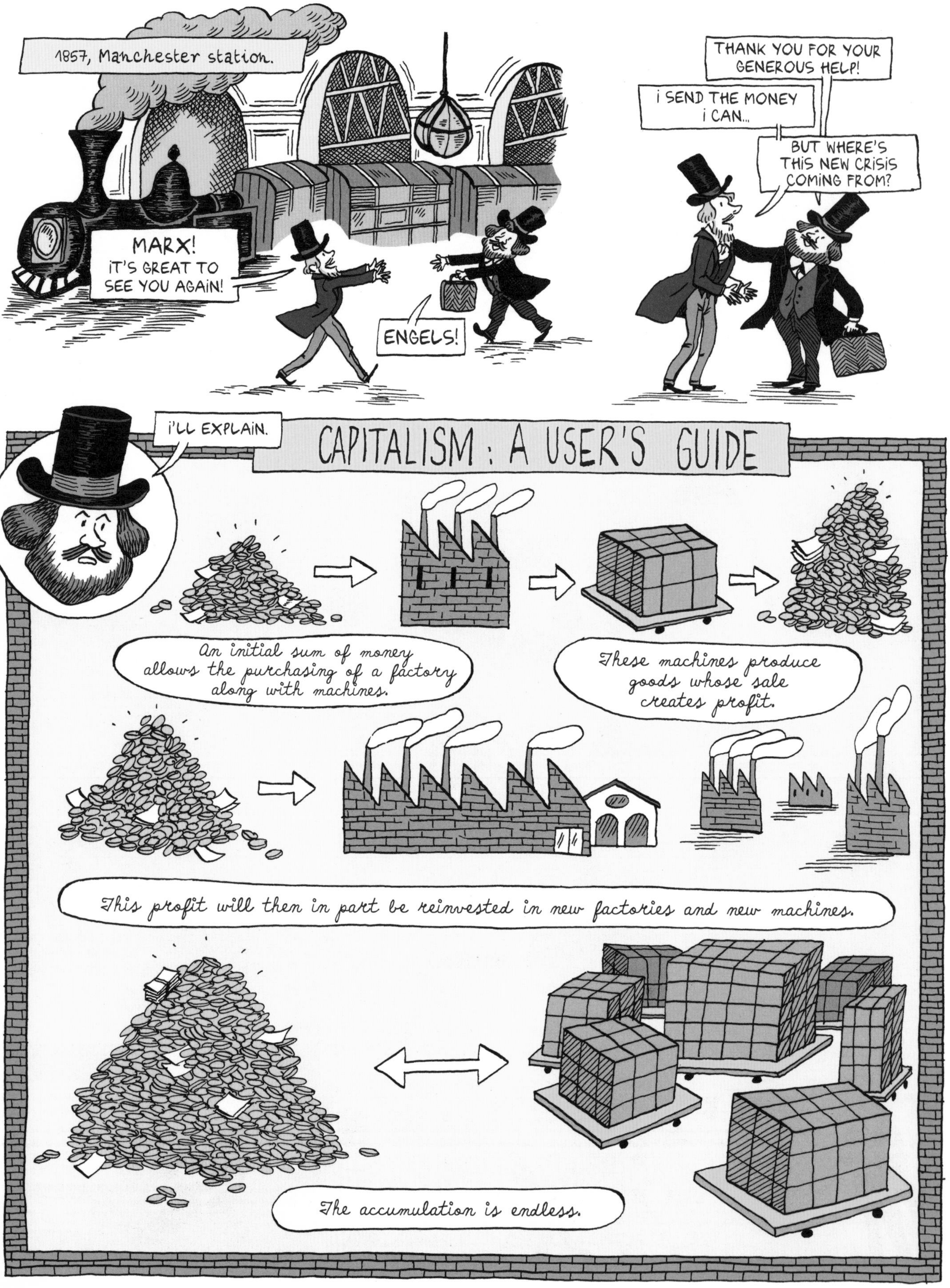
1857, Manchester station.
MARX! IT'S GREAT TO SEE YOU AGAIN!
ENGELS!
THANK YOU FOR YOUR GENEROUS HELP!
I SEND THE MONEY I CAN...
BUT WHERE'S THIS NEW CRISIS COMING FROM?
I'LL EXPLAIN.
CAPITALISM : A USER'S GUIDE
An initial sum of money allows the purchasing of a factory along with machines.
These machines produce goods whose sale creates profit.
This profit will then in part be reinvested in new factories and new machines.
The accumulation is endless.

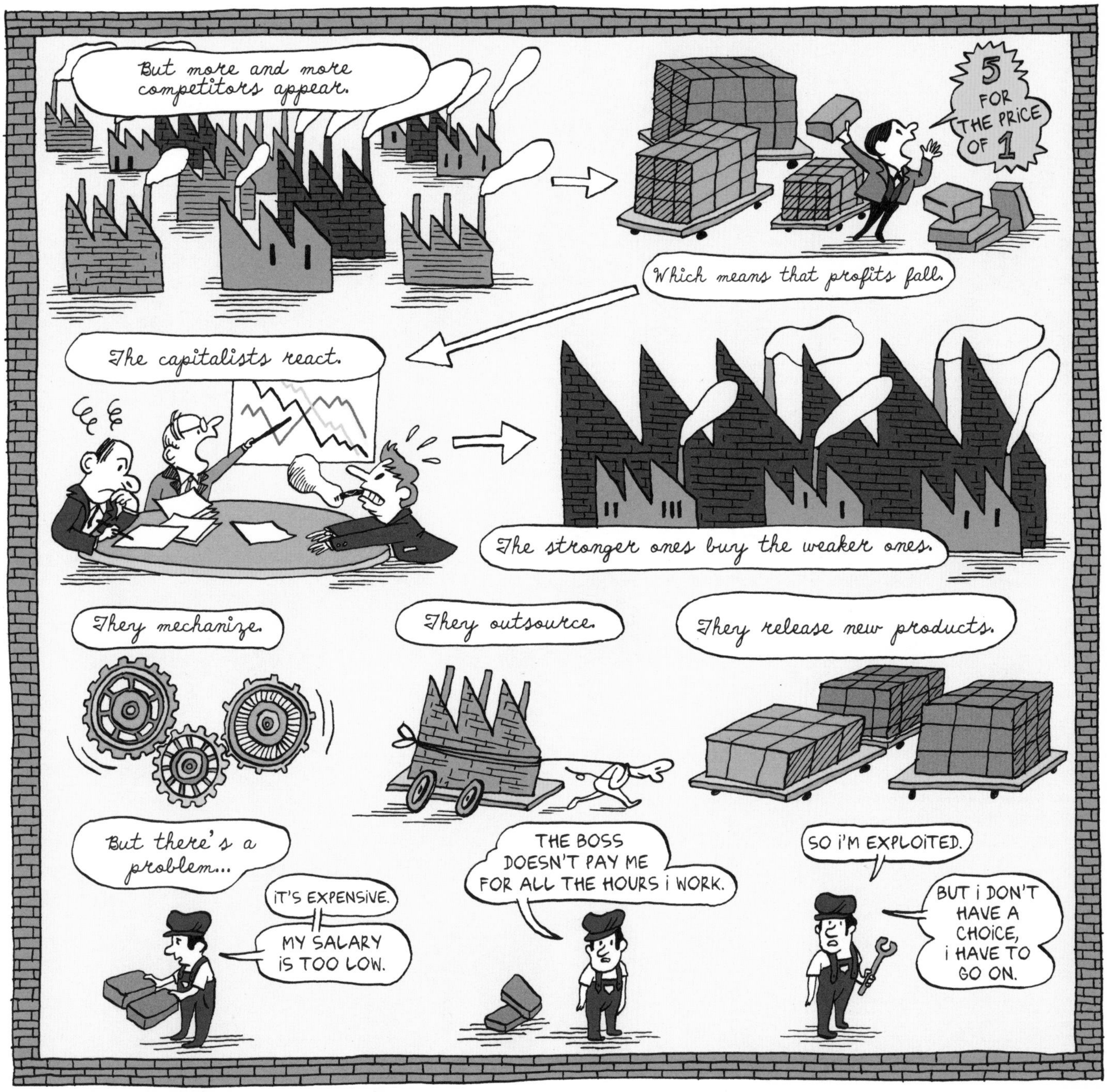
But more and more competitors appear.
5 FOR THE PRICE OF 1
Which means that profits fall.
The capitalists react.
The stronger ones buy the weaker ones.
They mechanize.
They outsource.
They release new products.
But there's a problem...
IT'S EXPENSIVE.
MY SALARY IS TOO LOW.
THE BOSS DOESN'T PAY ME FOR ALL THE HOURS I WORK.
SO I'M EXPLOITED.
BUT I DON'T HAVE A CHOICE, I HAVE TO GO ON.

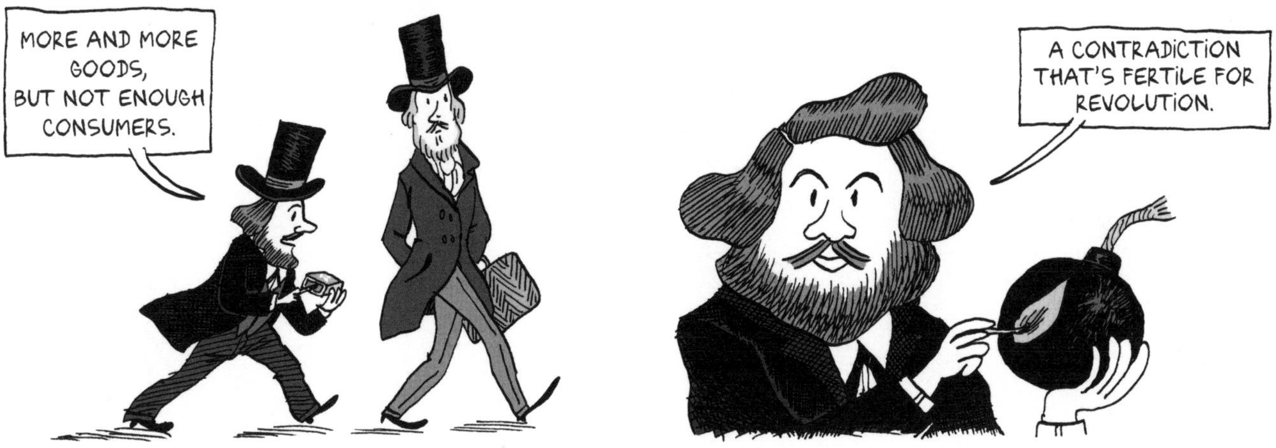
MORE AND MORE GOODS, BUT NOT ENOUGH CONSUMERS.
A CONTRADICTION THAT'S FERTILE FOR REVOLUTION.

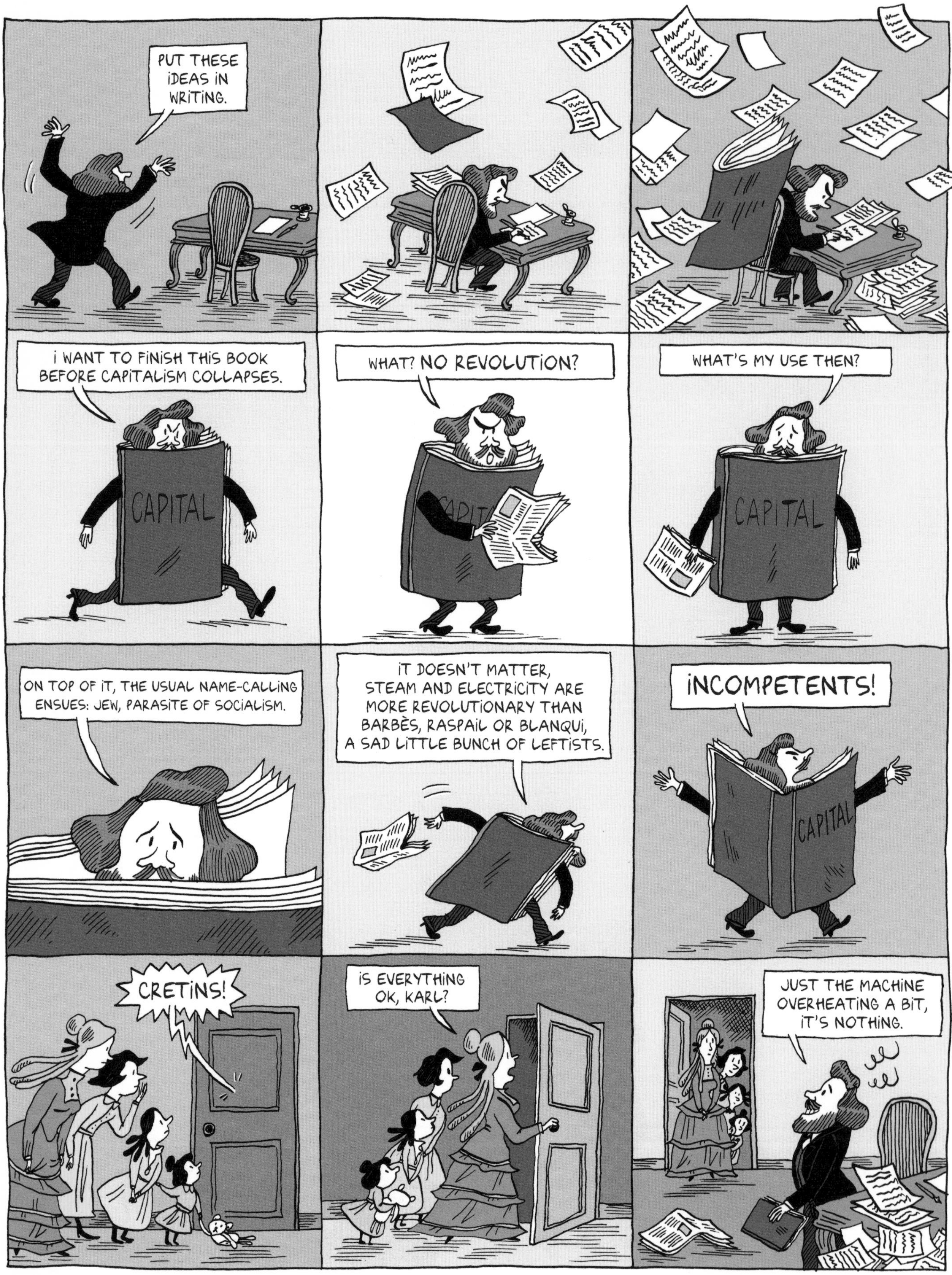

PUT THESE IDEAS IN WRITING.
I WANT TO FINISH THIS BOOK BEFORE CAPITALISM COLLAPSES.
CAPITAL
WHAT? NO REVOLUTION?
WHAT'S MY USE THEN?
CAPITAL
ON TOP OF IT, THE USUAL NAME-CALLING ENSUES: JEW, PARASITE OF SOCIALISM.
IT DOESN'T MATTER, STEAM AND ELECTRICITY ARE MORE REVOLUTIONARY THAN BARBÈS, RASPAIL OR BLANQUI, A SAD LITTLE BUNCH OF LEFTISTS.
INCOMPETENTS!
CAPITAL
CRETINS!
IS EVERYTHING OK, KARL?
JUST THE MACHINE OVERHEATING A BIT, IT'S NOTHING.

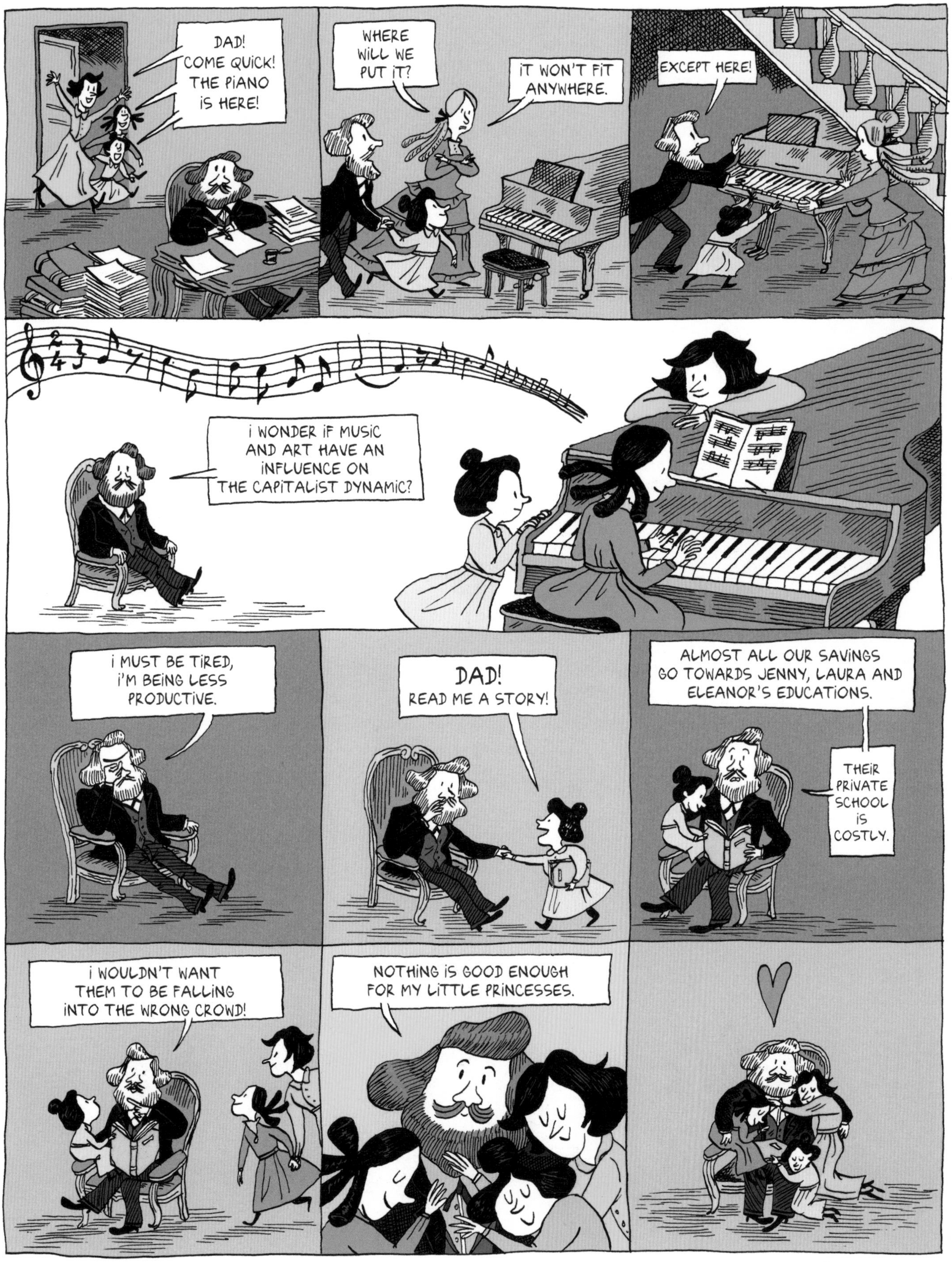
DAD! COME QUICK! THE PIANO IS HERE!
WHERE WILL WE PUT IT?
IT WON'T FIT ANYWHERE.
EXCEPT HERE!
I WONDER IF MUSIC AND ART HAVE AN INFLUENCE ON THE CAPITALIST DYNAMIC?
I MUST BE TIRED, I'M BEING LESS PRODUCTIVE.
DAD! READ ME A STORY!
ALMOST ALL OUR SAVINGS GO TOWARDS JENNY, LAURA AND ELEANOR'S EDUCATIONS.
THEIR PRIVATE SCHOOL IS COSTLY.
I WOULDN'T WANT THEM TO BE FALLING INTO THE WRONG CROWD!
NOTHING IS GOOD ENOUGH FOR MY LITTLE PRINCESSES.

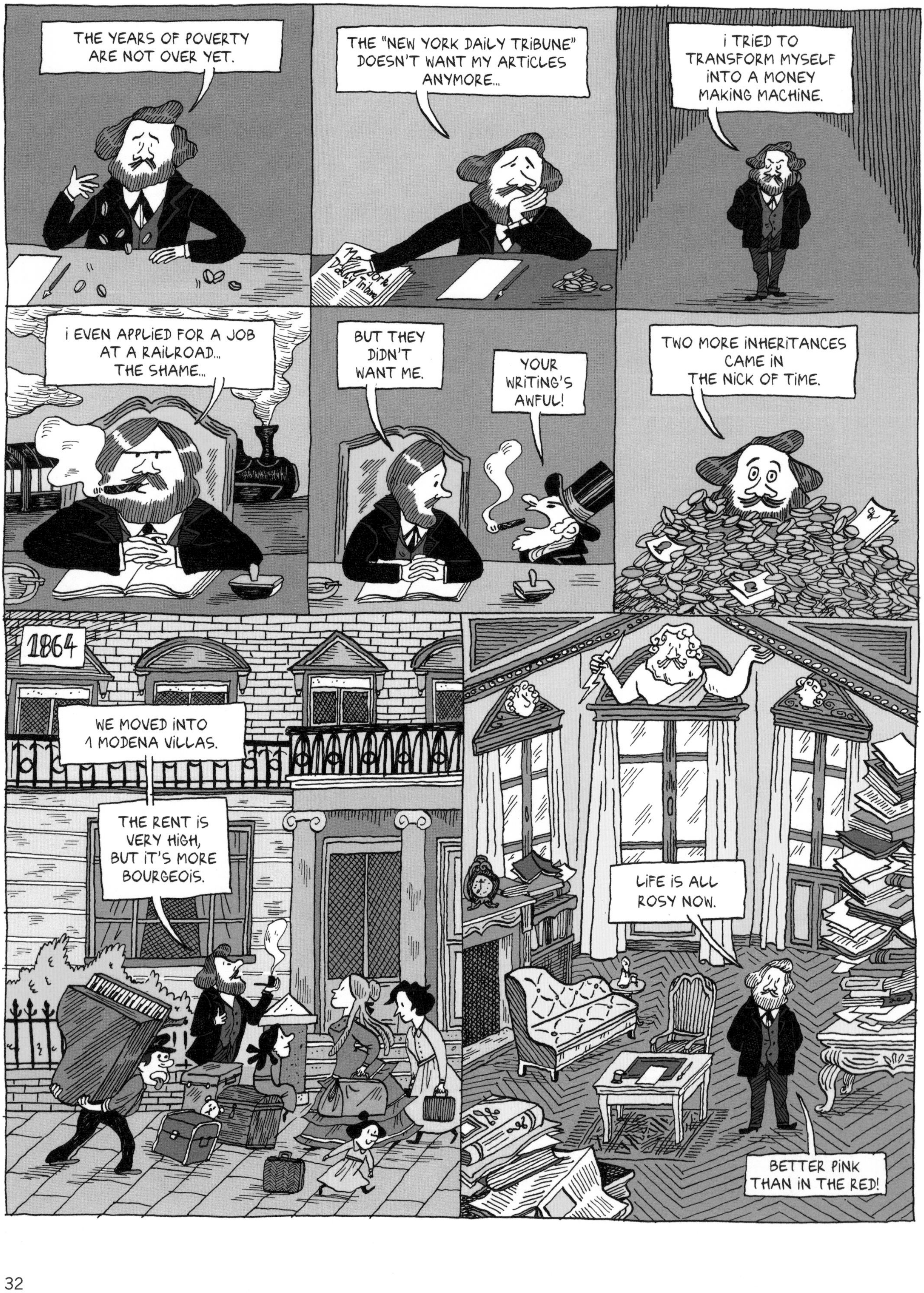
THE YEARS OF POVERTY ARE NOT OVER YET.
THE "NEW YORK DAILY TRIBUNE" DOESN'T WANT MY ARTICLES ANYMORE...
I TRIED TO TRANSFORM MYSELF INTO A MONEY MAKING MACHINE.
I EVEN APPLIED FOR A JOB AT A RAILROAD... THE SHAME...
BUT THEY DIDN'T WANT ME.
YOUR WRITING'S AWFUL!
TWO MORE INHERITANCES CAME IN THE NICK OF TIME.
1864
WE MOVED INTO 1 MODENA VILLAS.
THE RENT IS VERY HIGH, BUT IT'S MORE BOURGEOIS.
LIFE IS ALL ROSY NOW.
BETTER PINK THAN IN THE RED!

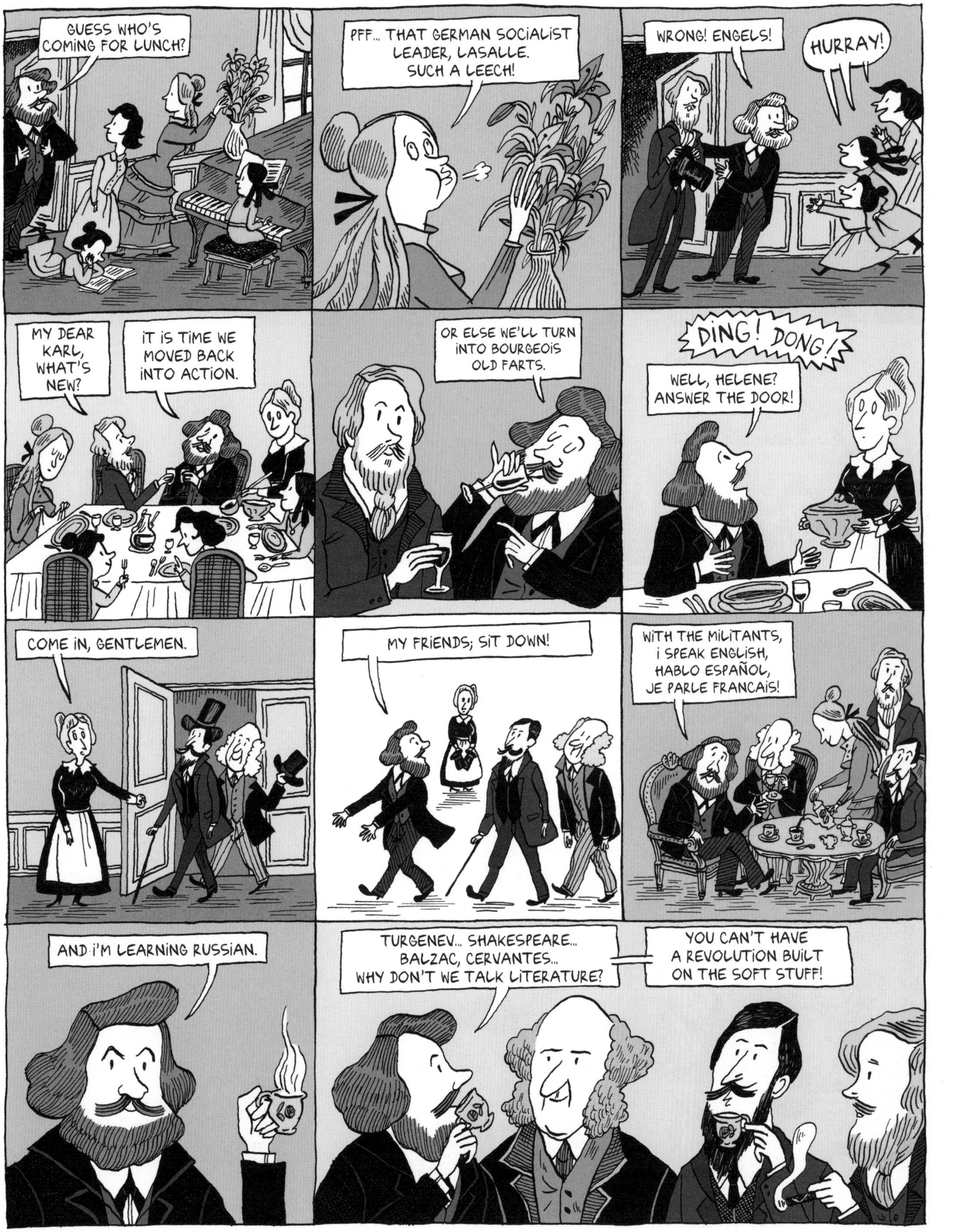
GUESS WHO'S COMING FOR LUNCH?
PFF... THAT GERMAN SOCIALIST LEADER, LASALLE. SUCH A LEECH!
WRONG! ENGELS!
HURRAY!
MY DEAR KARL, WHAT'S NEW?
IT IS TIME WE MOVED BACK INTO ACTION.
OR ELSE WE'LL TURN INTO BOURGEOIS OLD FARTS.
DING! DONG!
WELL, HELENE? ANSWER THE DOOR!
COME IN, GENTLEMEN.
MY FRIENDS; SIT DOWN!
WITH THE MILITANTS, I SPEAK ENGLISH, HABLO ESPAÑOL, JE PARLE FRANCAIS!
AND I'M LEARNING RUSSIAN.
TURGENEV... SHAKESPEARE... BALZAC, CERVANTES... WHY DON'T WE TALK LITERATURE?
YOU CAN'T HAVE A REVOLUTION BUILT ON THE SOFT STUFF!

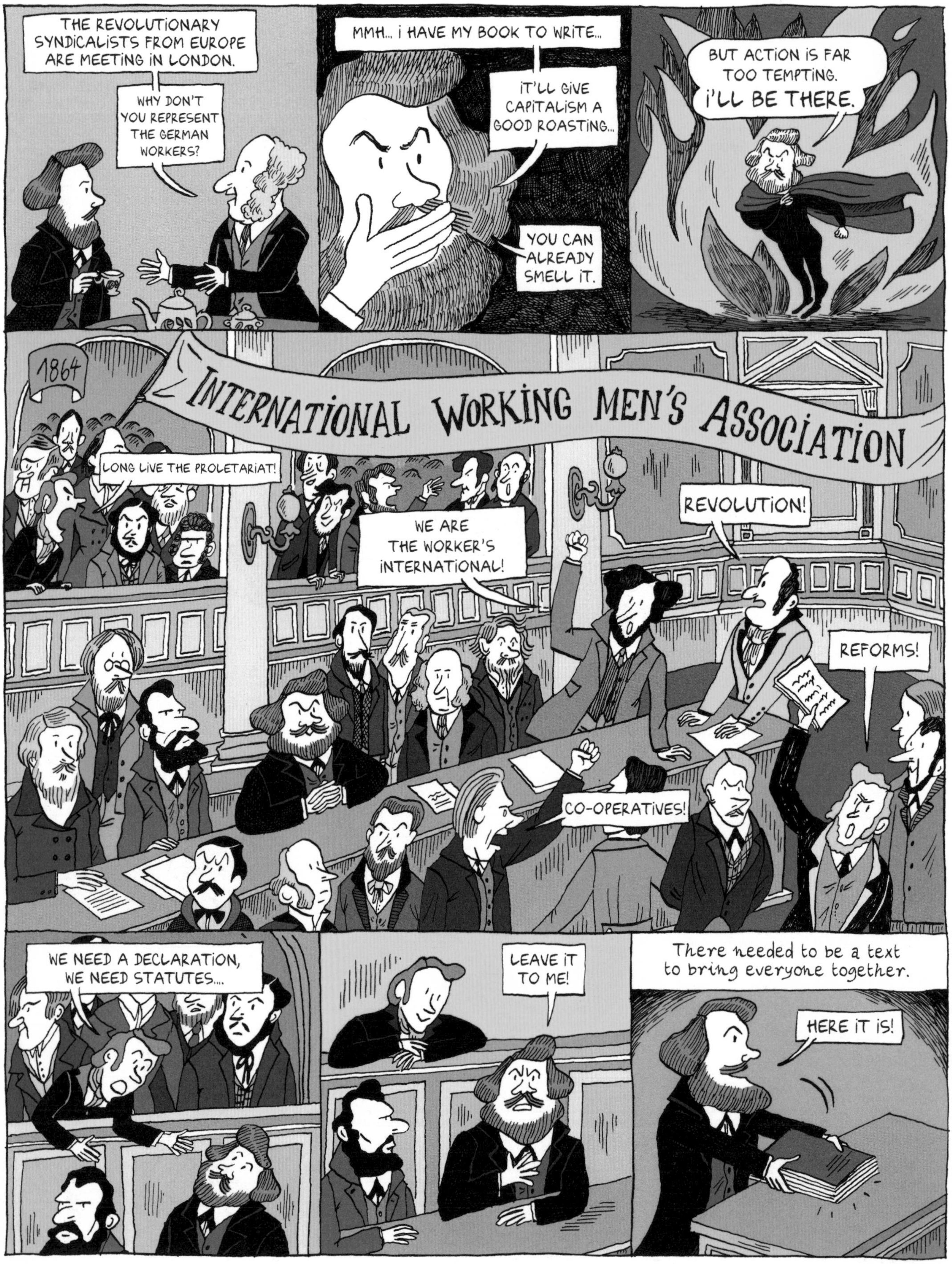
THE REVOLUTIONARY SYNDICALISTS FROM EUROPE ARE MEETING IN LONDON.
WHY DON'T YOU REPRESENT THE GERMAN WORKERS?
MMH... I HAVE MY BOOK TO WRITE...
IT'LL GIVE CAPITALISM A GOOD ROASTING...
YOU CAN ALREADY SMELL IT.
BUT ACTION IS FAR TOO TEMPTING.
I'LL BE THERE.
1864
INTERNATIONAL WORKING MEN'S ASSOCIATION
LONG LIVE THE PROLETARIAT!
WE ARE THE WORKER'S INTERNATIONAL!
REVOLUTION!
REFORMS!
CO-OPERATIVES!
WE NEED A DECLARATION, WE NEED STATUTES....
LEAVE IT TO ME!
There needed to be a text to bring everyone together.
HERE IT IS!

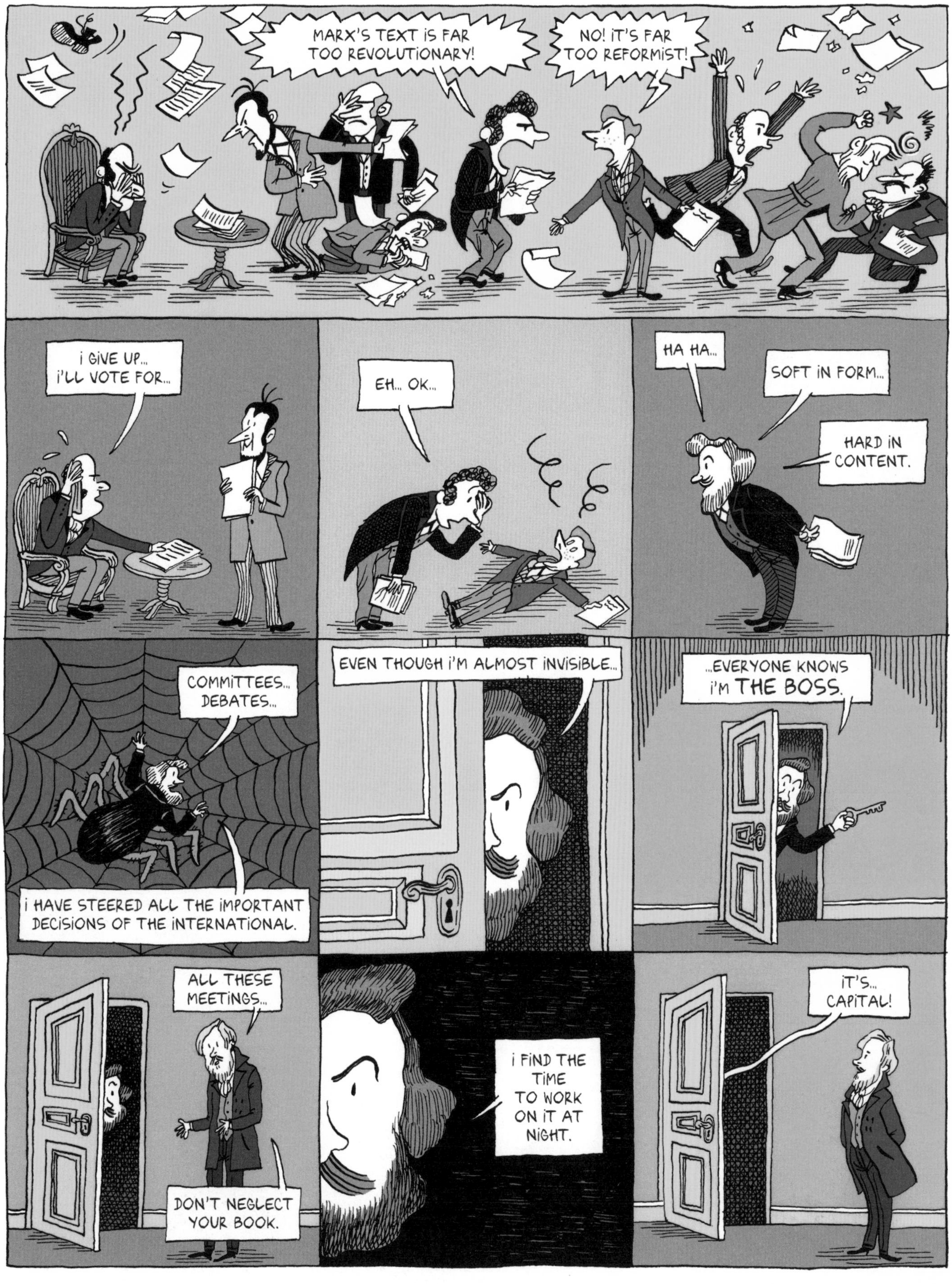
MARX'S TEXT IS FAR TOO REVOLUTIONARY!
NO! IT'S FAR TOO REFORMIST!
I GIVE UP... I'LL VOTE FOR...
EH... OK...
HA HA...
SOFT IN FORM...
HARD IN CONTENT.
COMMITTEES... DEBATES...
I HAVE STEERED ALL THE IMPORTANT DECISIONS OF THE INTERNATIONAL.
EVEN THOUGH I'M ALMOST INVISIBLE...
...EVERYONE KNOWS I'M THE BOSS.
ALL THESE MEETINGS...
DON'T NEGLECT YOUR BOOK.
I FIND THE TIME TO WORK ON IT AT NIGHT.
IT'S... CAPITAL!

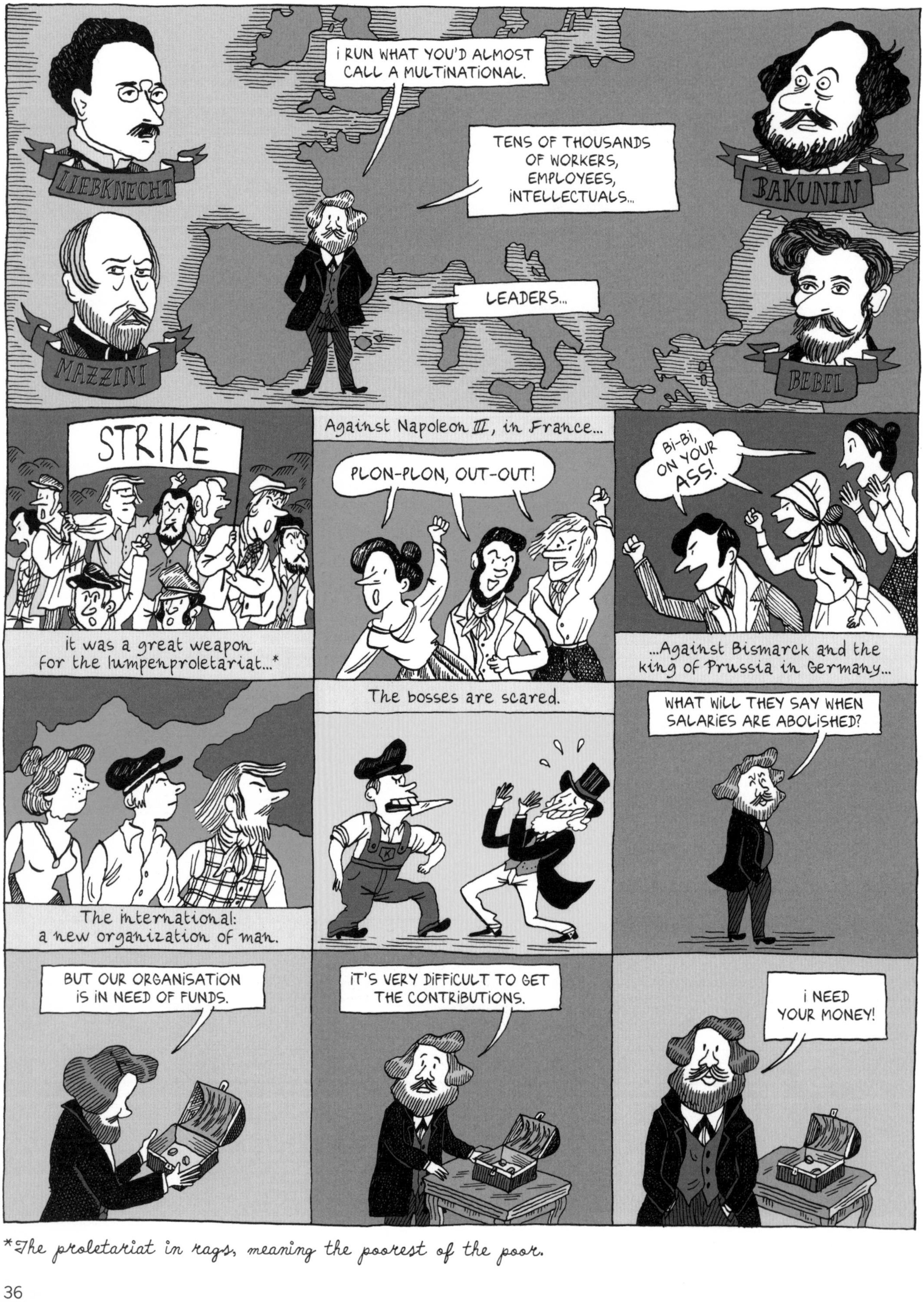
LIEBKNECHT
MAZZINI
BAKUNIN
BEBEL
I RUN WHAT YOU'D ALMOST CALL A MULTINATIONAL.
TENS OF THOUSANDS OF WORKERS, EMPLOYEES, INTELLECTUALS...
LEADERS...
STRIKE
it was a great weapon for the lumpenproletariat...*
Against Napoleon III, in France...
PLON-PLON, OUT-OUT!
BI-BI, ON YOUR ASS!
...Against Bismarck and the king of Prussia in Germany...
The international: a new organization of man.
The bosses are scared.
WHAT WILL THEY SAY WHEN SALARIES ARE ABOLISHED?
BUT OUR ORGANISATION IS IN NEED OF FUNDS.
IT'S VERY DIFFICULT TO GET THE CONTRIBUTIONS.
I NEED YOUR MONEY!

*The proletariat in rags, meaning the poorest of the poor.

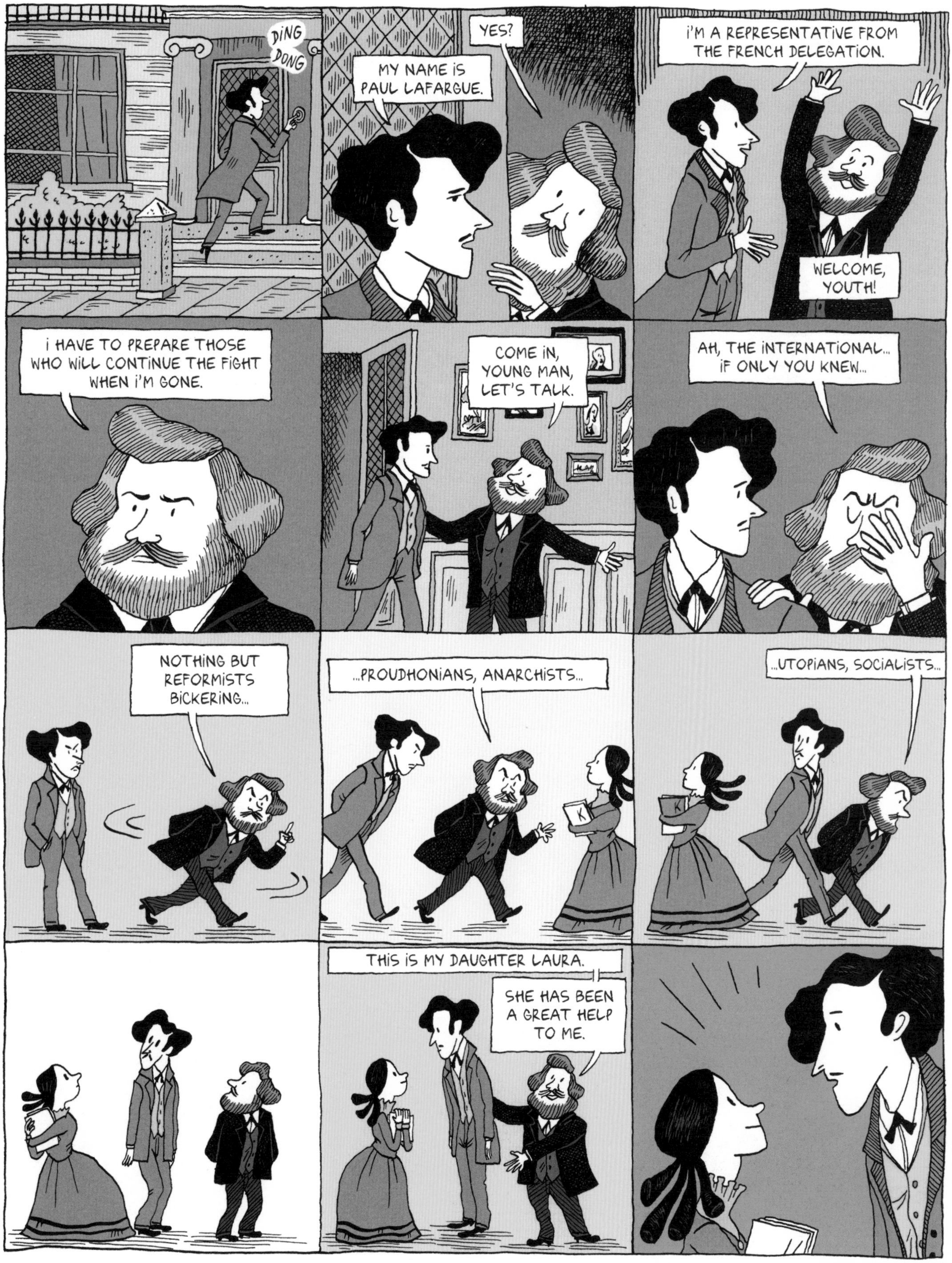
DING DONG
MY NAME IS PAUL LAFARGUE.
YES?
I'M A REPRESENTATIVE FROM THE FRENCH DELEGATION.
WELCOME, YOUTH!
I HAVE TO PREPARE THOSE WHO WILL CONTINUE THE FIGHT WHEN I'M GONE.
COME IN, YOUNG MAN, LET'S TALK.
AH, THE INTERNATIONAL... IF ONLY YOU KNEW...
NOTHING BUT REFORMISTS BICKERING...
...PROUDHONIANS, ANARCHISTS...
...UTOPIANS, SOCIALISTS...
THIS IS MY DAUGHTER LAURA.
SHE HAS BEEN A GREAT HELP TO ME.

CAPITAL - *Volume 1* - 1867

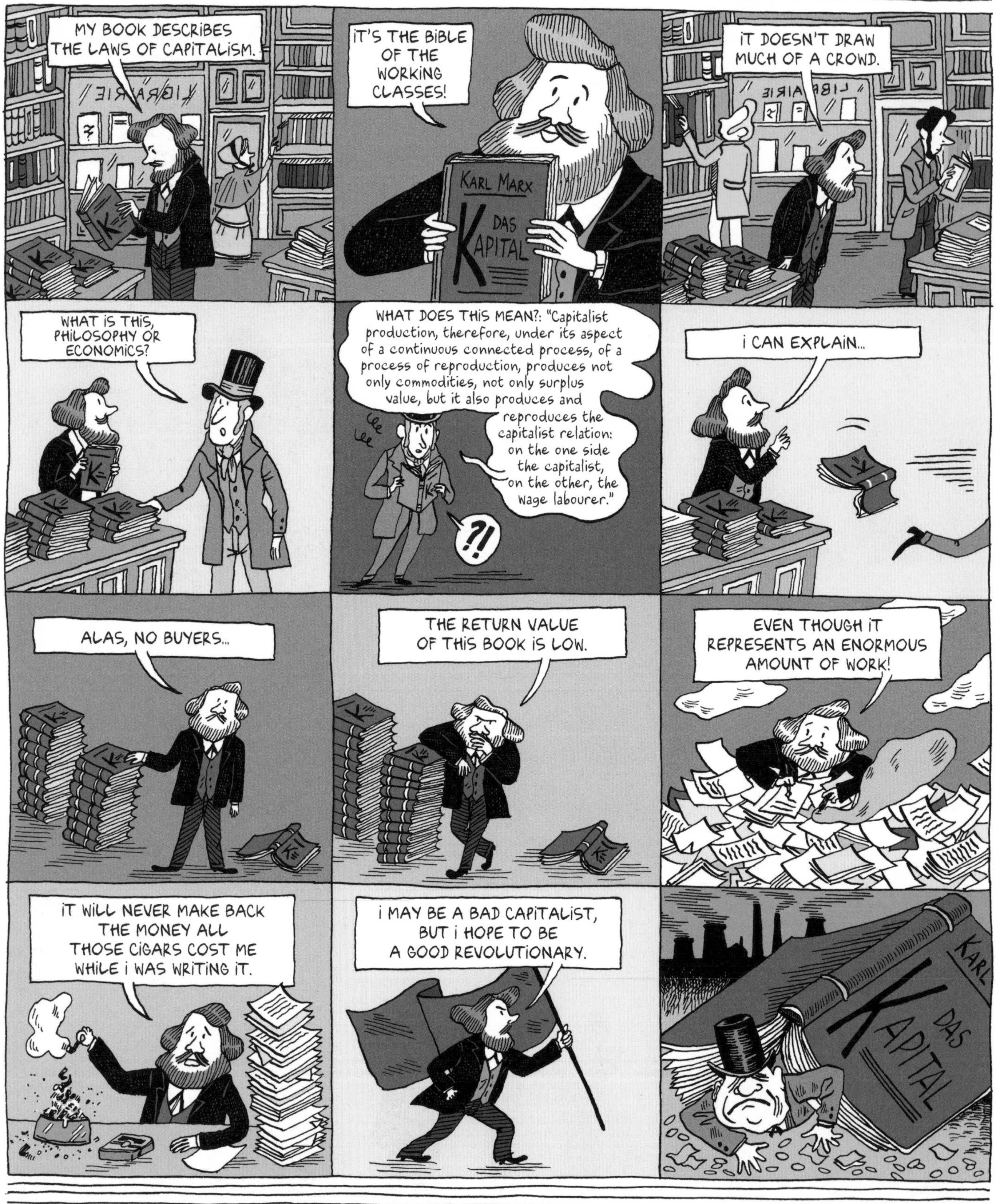
MY BOOK DESCRIBES THE LAWS OF CAPITALISM.
LIBRAIRIE
IT'S THE BIBLE OF THE WORKING CLASSES!
KARL MARX DAS KAPITAL
IT DOESN'T DRAW MUCH OF A CROWD.
LIBRAIRIE
WHAT IS THIS, PHILOSOPHY OR ECONOMICS?
WHAT DOES THIS MEAN?: "Capitalist production, therefore, under its aspect of a continuous connected process, of a process of reproduction, produces not only commodities, not only surplus value, but it also produces and reproduces the capitalist relation: on the one side the capitalist, on the other, the wage labourer."
?!
I CAN EXPLAIN...
ALAS, NO BUYERS...
THE RETURN VALUE OF THIS BOOK IS LOW.
EVEN THOUGH IT REPRESENTS AN ENORMOUS AMOUNT OF WORK!
IT WILL NEVER MAKE BACK THE MONEY ALL THOSE CIGARS COST ME WHILE I WAS WRITING IT.
I MAY BE A BAD CAPITALIST, BUT I HOPE TO BE A GOOD REVOLUTIONARY.
KARL DAS KAPITAL

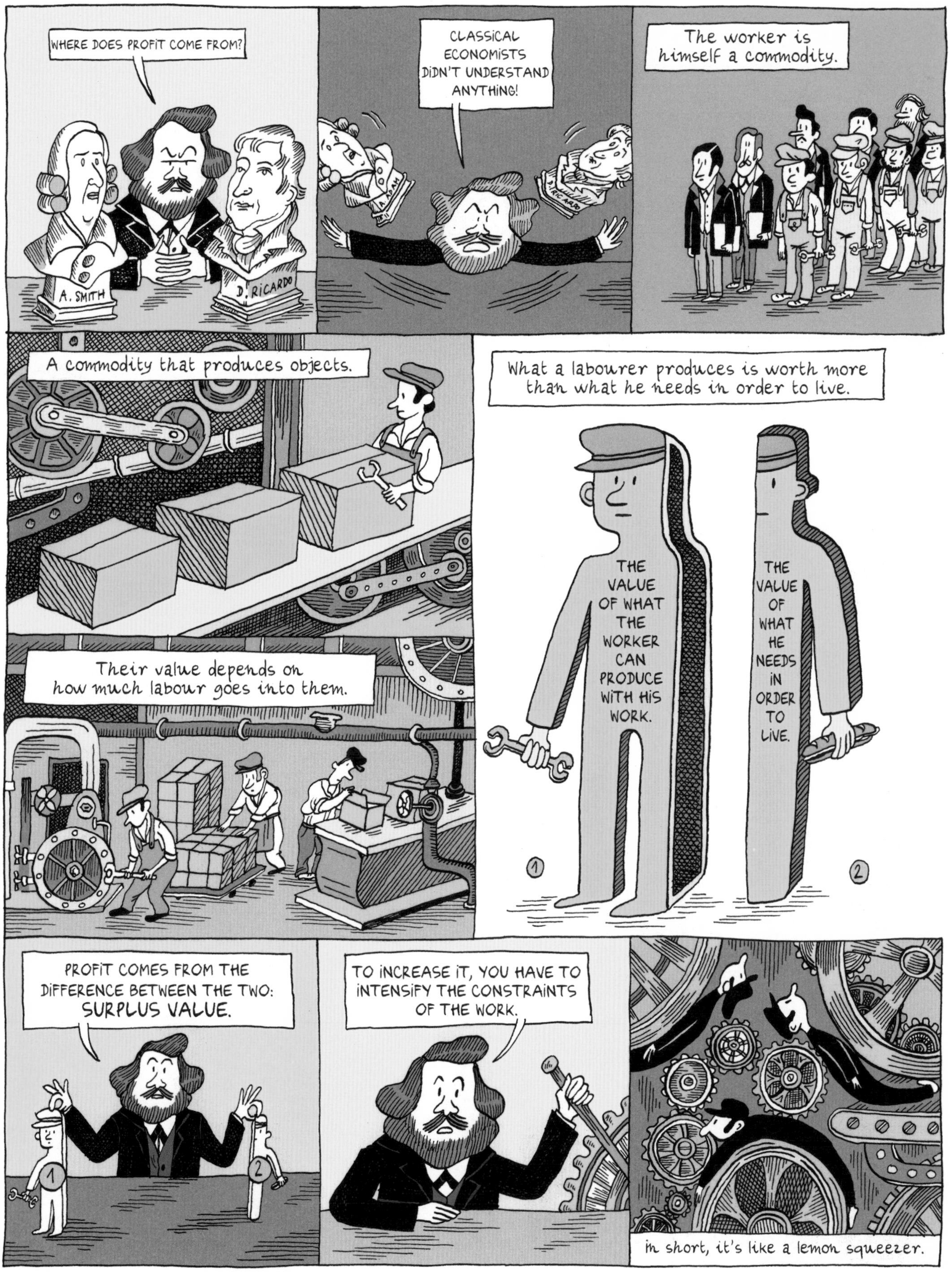
WHERE DOES PROFIT COME FROM?
A. SMITH
D. RICARDO
CLASSICAL ECONOMISTS DIDN'T UNDERSTAND ANYTHING!
The worker is himself a commodity.
A commodity that produces objects.
Their value depends on how much labour goes into them.
What a labourer produces is worth more than what he needs in order to live.
THE VALUE OF WHAT THE WORKER CAN PRODUCE WITH HIS WORK.
THE VALUE OF WHAT HE NEEDS IN ORDER TO LIVE.
1
2
PROFIT COMES FROM THE DIFFERENCE BETWEEN THE TWO: SURPLUS VALUE.
TO INCREASE IT, YOU HAVE TO INTENSIFY THE CONSTRAINTS OF THE WORK.
In short, it's like a lemon squeezer.

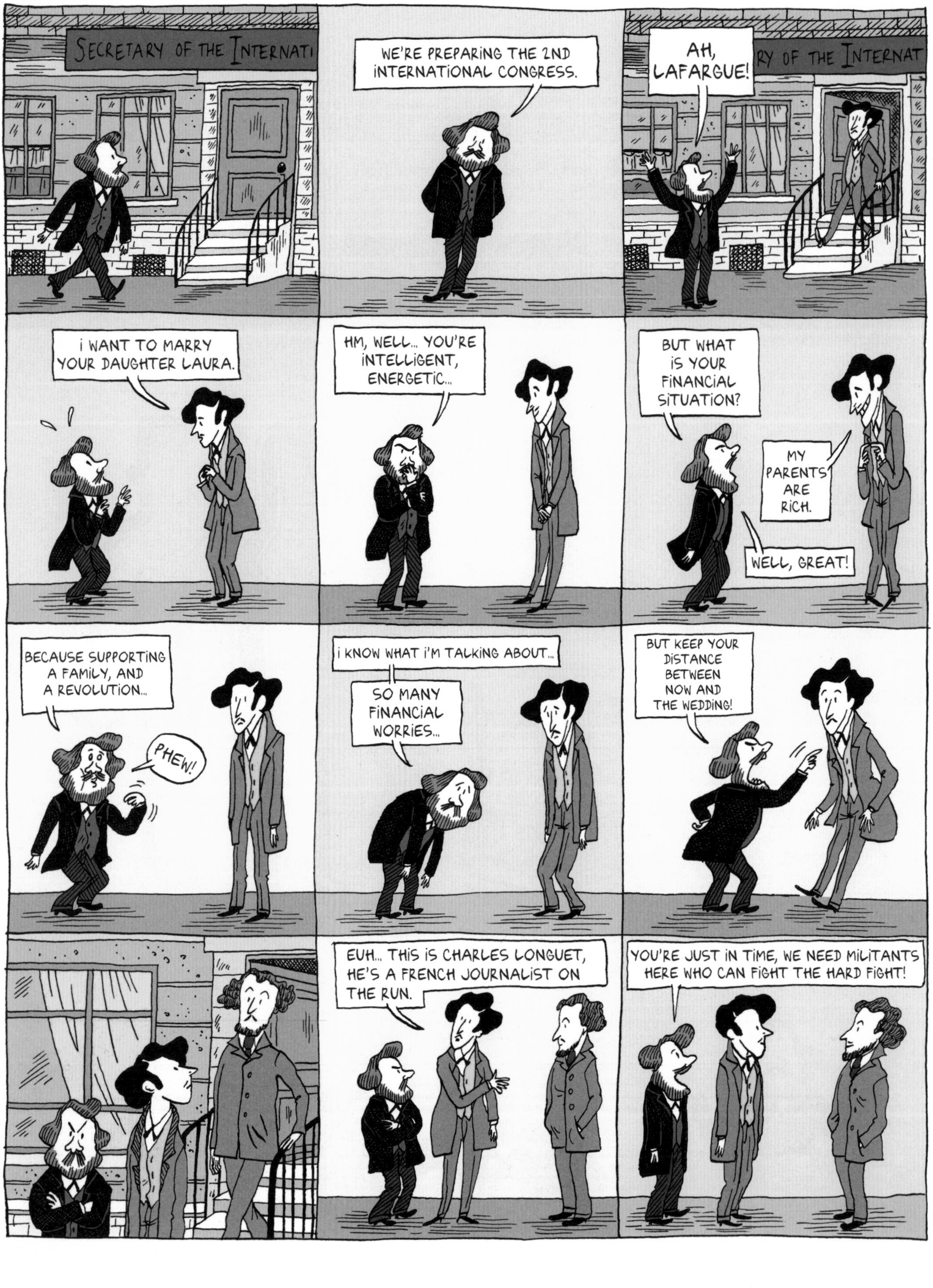
SECRETARY OF THE INTERNATI
WE'RE PREPARING THE 2ND INTERNATIONAL CONGRESS.
AH, LAFARGUE!
RY OF THE INTERNAT
I WANT TO MARRY YOUR DAUGHTER LAURA.
HM, WELL... YOU'RE INTELLIGENT, ENERGETIC...
BUT WHAT IS YOUR FINANCIAL SITUATION?
MY PARENTS ARE RICH.
WELL, GREAT!
BECAUSE SUPPORTING A FAMILY, AND A REVOLUTION...
PHEW!
I KNOW WHAT I'M TALKING ABOUT...
SO MANY FINANCIAL WORRIES...
BUT KEEP YOUR DISTANCE BETWEEN NOW AND THE WEDDING!
EUH... THIS IS CHARLES LONGUET, HE'S A FRENCH JOURNALIST ON THE RUN.
YOU'RE JUST IN TIME, WE NEED MILITANTS HERE WHO CAN FIGHT THE HARD FIGHT!

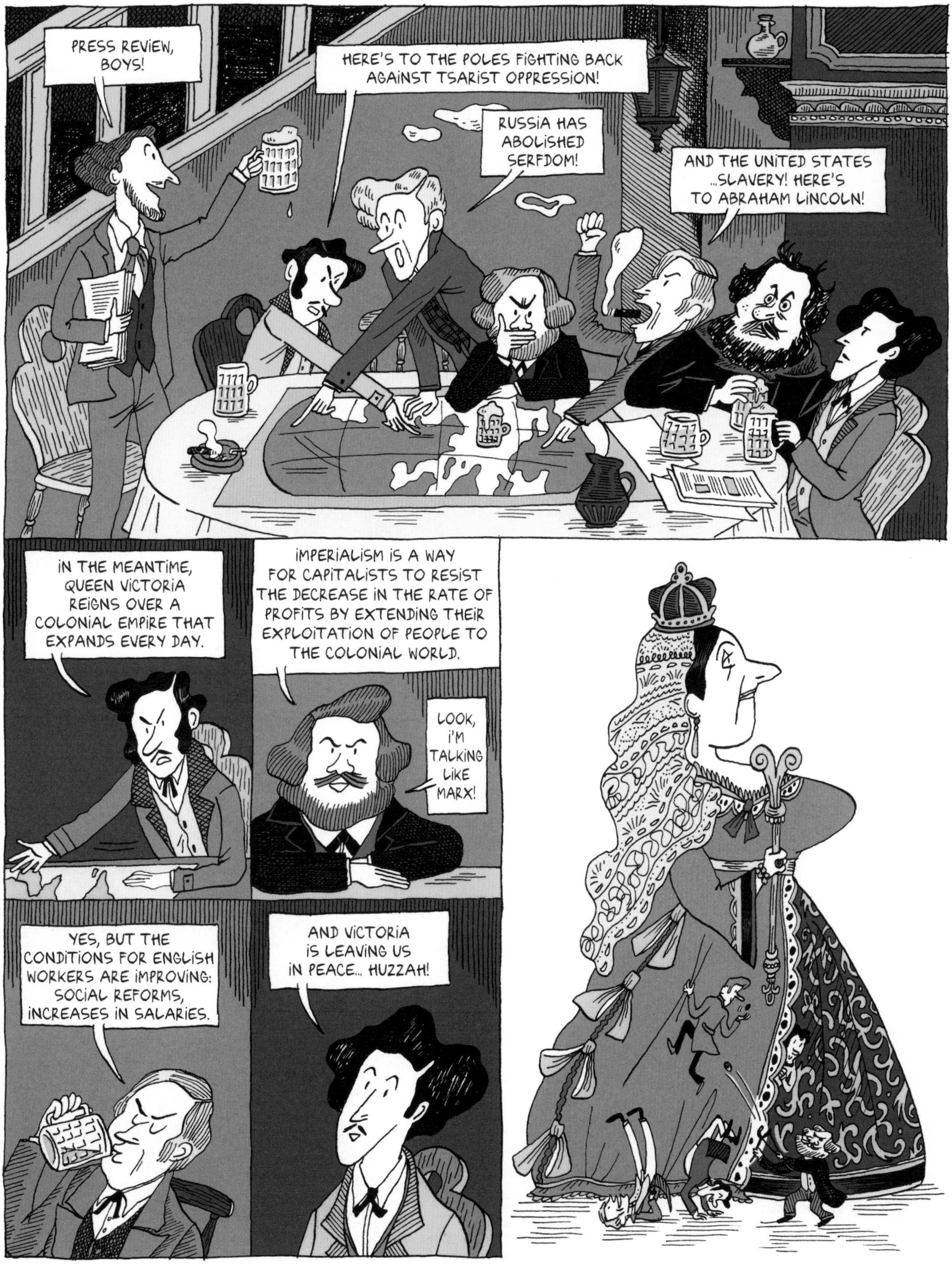

PRESS REVIEW, BOYS!
HERE'S TO THE POLES FIGHTING BACK AGAINST TSARIST OPPRESSION!
RUSSIA HAS ABOLISHED SERFDOM!
AND THE UNITED STATES ...SLAVERY! HERE'S TO ABRAHAM LINCOLN!
IN THE MEANTIME, QUEEN VICTORIA REIGNS OVER A COLONIAL EMPIRE THAT EXPANDS EVERY DAY.
IMPERIALISM IS A WAY FOR CAPITALISTS TO RESIST THE DECREASE IN THE RATE OF PROFITS BY EXTENDING THEIR EXPLOITATION OF PEOPLE TO THE COLONIAL WORLD.
LOOK, I'M TALKING LIKE MARX!
YES, BUT THE CONDITIONS FOR ENGLISH WORKERS ARE IMPROVING: SOCIAL REFORMS, INCREASES IN SALARIES.
AND VICTORIA IS LEAVING US IN PEACE... HUZZAH!

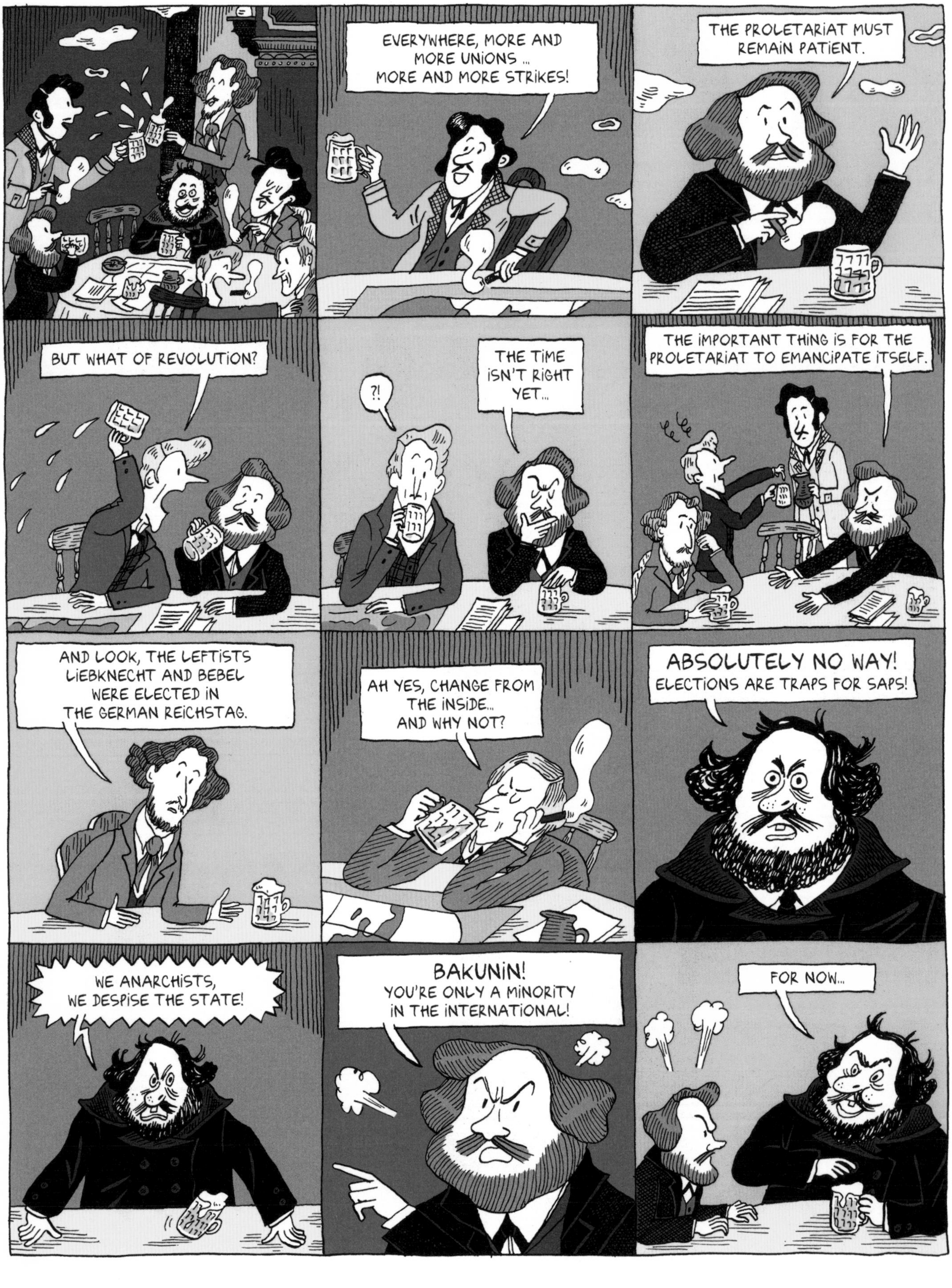
EVERYWHERE, MORE AND MORE UNIONS ... MORE AND MORE STRIKES!
THE PROLETARIAT MUST REMAIN PATIENT.
BUT WHAT OF REVOLUTION?
?!
THE TIME ISN'T RIGHT YET...
THE IMPORTANT THING IS FOR THE PROLETARIAT TO EMANCIPATE ITSELF.
AND LOOK, THE LEFTISTS LIEBKNECHT AND BEBEL WERE ELECTED IN THE GERMAN REICHSTAG.
AH YES, CHANGE FROM THE INSIDE... AND WHY NOT?
ABSOLUTELY NO WAY!
ELECTIONS ARE TRAPS FOR SAPS!
WE ANARCHISTS, WE DESPISE THE STATE!
BAKUNIN!
YOU'RE ONLY A MINORITY IN THE INTERNATIONAL!
FOR NOW...

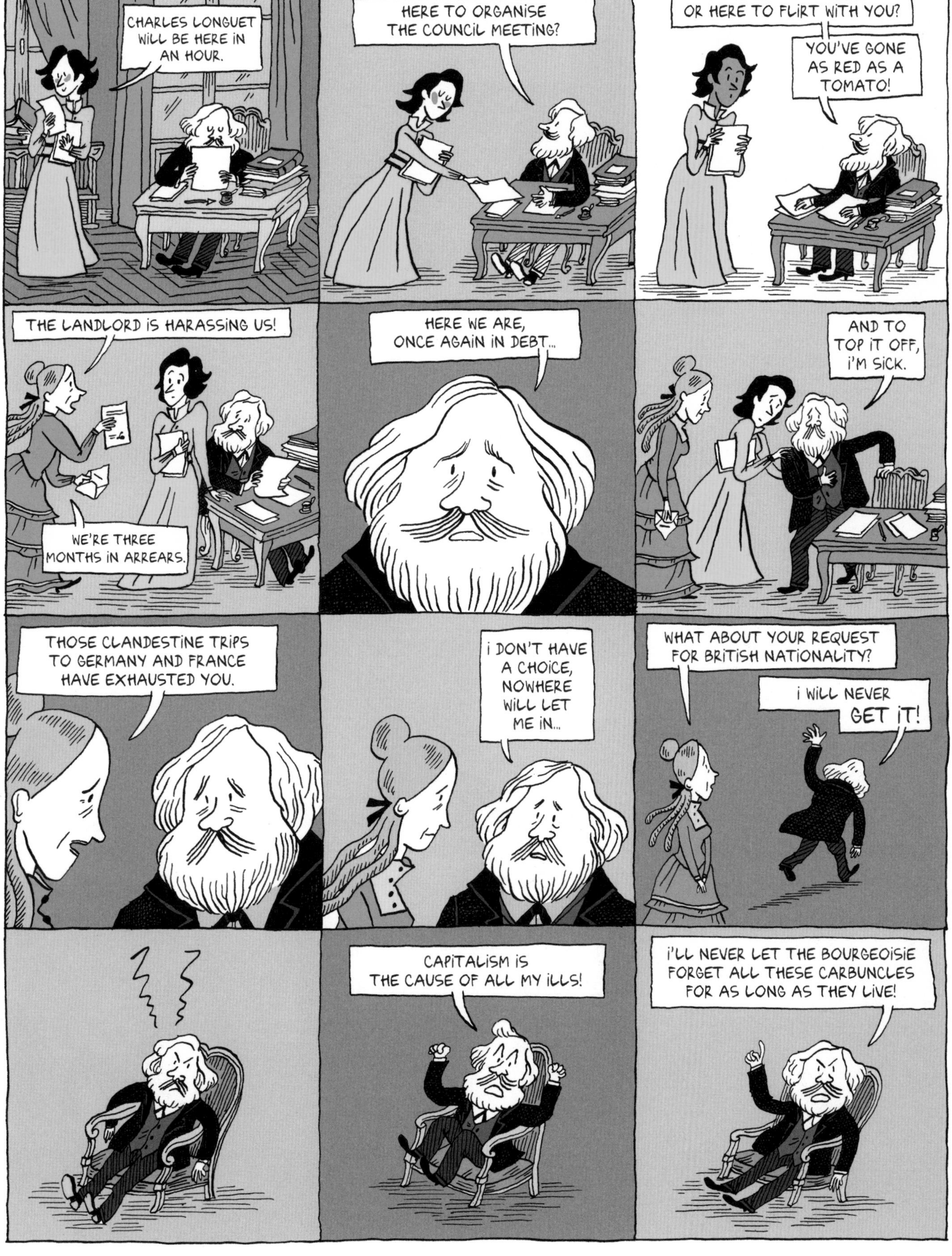
CHARLES LONGUET WILL BE HERE IN AN HOUR.
HERE TO ORGANISE THE COUNCIL MEETING?
OR HERE TO FLIRT WITH YOU?
YOU'VE GONE AS RED AS A TOMATO!
THE LANDLORD IS HARASSING US!
WE'RE THREE MONTHS IN ARREARS.
HERE WE ARE, ONCE AGAIN IN DEBT...
AND TO TOP IT OFF, I'M SICK.
THOSE CLANDESTINE TRIPS TO GERMANY AND FRANCE HAVE EXHAUSTED YOU.
I DON'T HAVE A CHOICE, NOWHERE WILL LET ME IN...
WHAT ABOUT YOUR REQUEST FOR BRITISH NATIONALITY?
I WILL NEVER GET IT!
CAPITALISM IS THE CAUSE OF ALL MY ILLS!
I'LL NEVER LET THE BOURGEOISIE FORGET ALL THESE CARBUNCLES FOR AS LONG AS THEY LIVE!

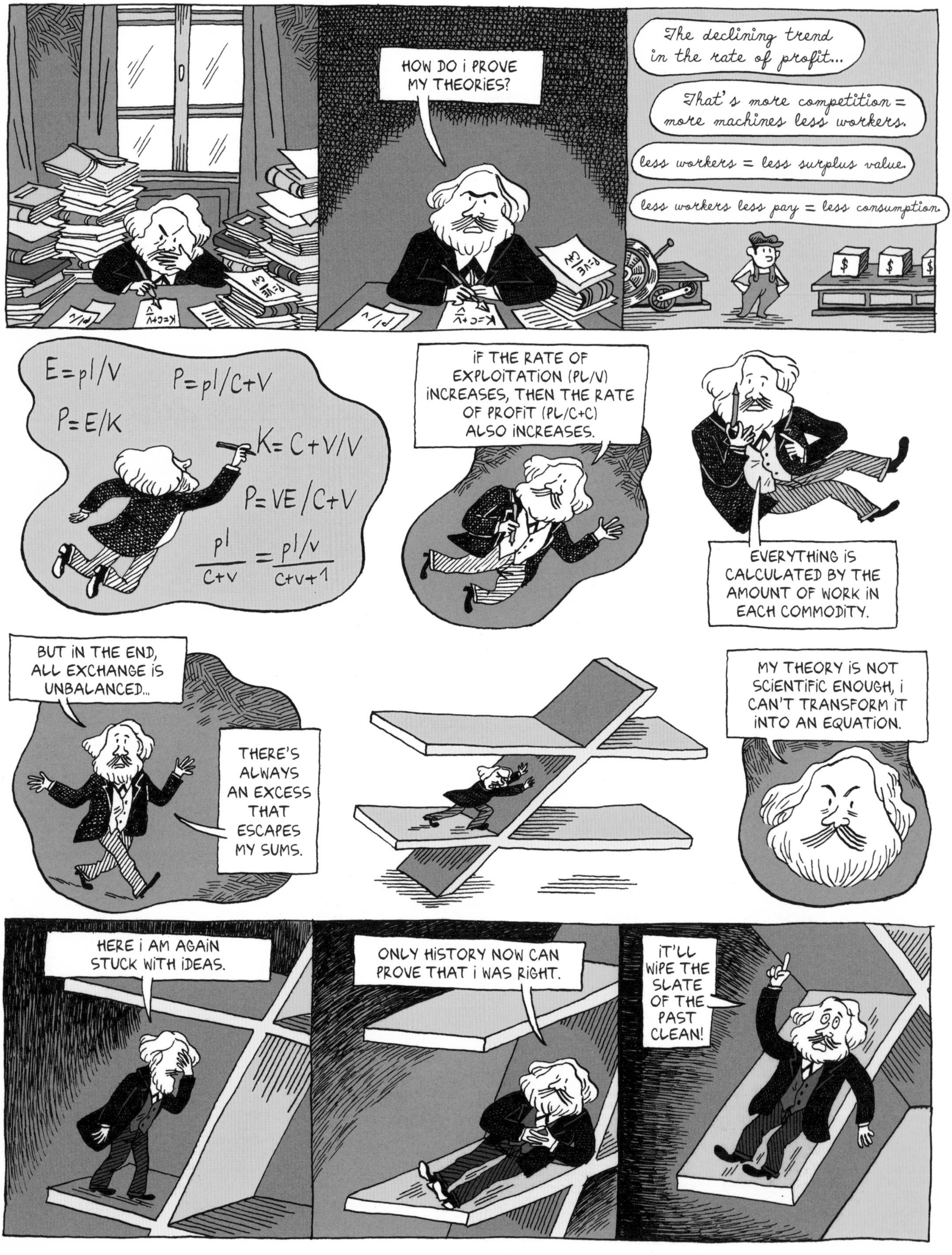
HOW DO I PROVE MY THEORIES?
The declining trend in the rate of profit...
That's more competition = more machines less workers.
less workers = less surplus value.
less workers less pay = less consumption.
E=pl/V
P=pl/C+V
P=E/K
K=C+V/V
P=VE/C+V
pl/C+V = pl/v / C+V+1
IF THE RATE OF EXPLOITATION (PL/V) INCREASES, THEN THE RATE OF PROFIT (PL/C+C) ALSO INCREASES.
EVERYTHING IS CALCULATED BY THE AMOUNT OF WORK IN EACH COMMODITY.
BUT IN THE END, ALL EXCHANGE IS UNBALANCED...
THERE'S ALWAYS AN EXCESS THAT ESCAPES MY SUMS.
MY THEORY IS NOT SCIENTIFIC ENOUGH, I CAN'T TRANSFORM IT INTO AN EQUATION.
HERE I AM AGAIN STUCK WITH IDEAS.
ONLY HISTORY NOW CAN PROVE THAT I WAS RIGHT.
IT'LL WIPE THE SLATE OF THE PAST CLEAN!

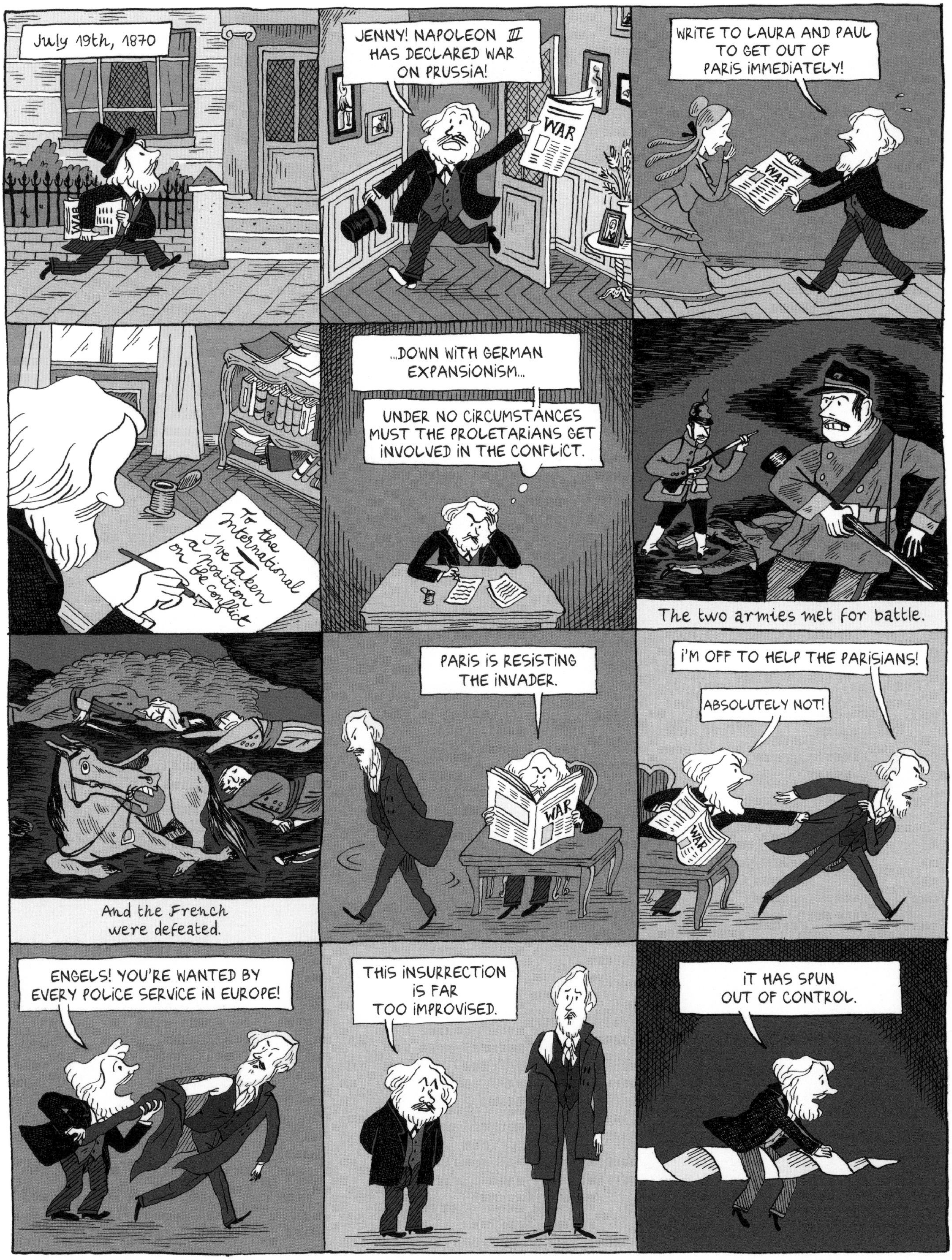
July 19th, 1870
JENNY! NAPOLEON III HAS DECLARED WAR ON PRUSSIA!
WAR
WRITE TO LAURA AND PAUL TO GET OUT OF PARIS IMMEDIATELY!
WAR
To the International I've taken a position on the conflict
...DOWN WITH GERMAN EXPANSIONISM...
UNDER NO CIRCUMSTANCES MUST THE PROLETARIANS GET INVOLVED IN THE CONFLICT.
The two armies met for battle.
And the French were defeated.
PARIS IS RESISTING THE INVADER.
WAR
I'M OFF TO HELP THE PARISIANS!
ABSOLUTELY NOT!
WAR
ENGELS! YOU'RE WANTED BY EVERY POLICE SERVICE IN EUROPE!
THIS INSURRECTION IS FAR TOO IMPROVISED.
IT HAS SPUN OUT OF CONTROL.

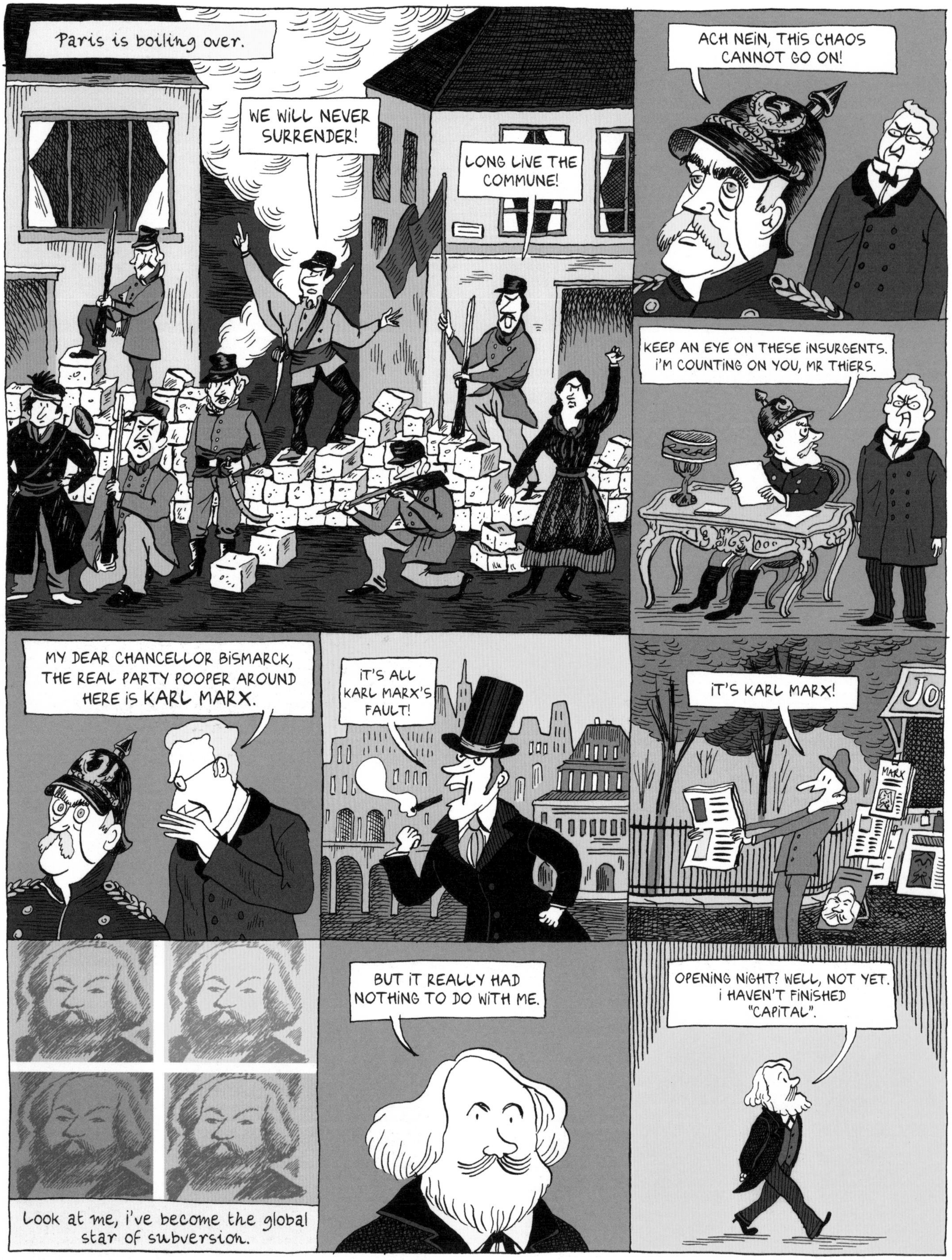

Paris is boiling over.
WE WILL NEVER SURRENDER!
LONG LIVE THE COMMUNE!
ACH NEIN, THIS CHAOS CANNOT GO ON!
KEEP AN EYE ON THESE INSURGENTS. I'M COUNTING ON YOU, MR THIERS.
MY DEAR CHANCELLOR BISMARCK, THE REAL PARTY POOPER AROUND HERE IS KARL MARX.
IT'S ALL KARL MARX'S FAULT!
IT'S KARL MARX!
MARX
Look at me, I've become the global star of subversion.
BUT IT REALLY HAD NOTHING TO DO WITH ME.
OPENING NIGHT? WELL, NOT YET. I HAVEN'T FINISHED "CAPITAL".

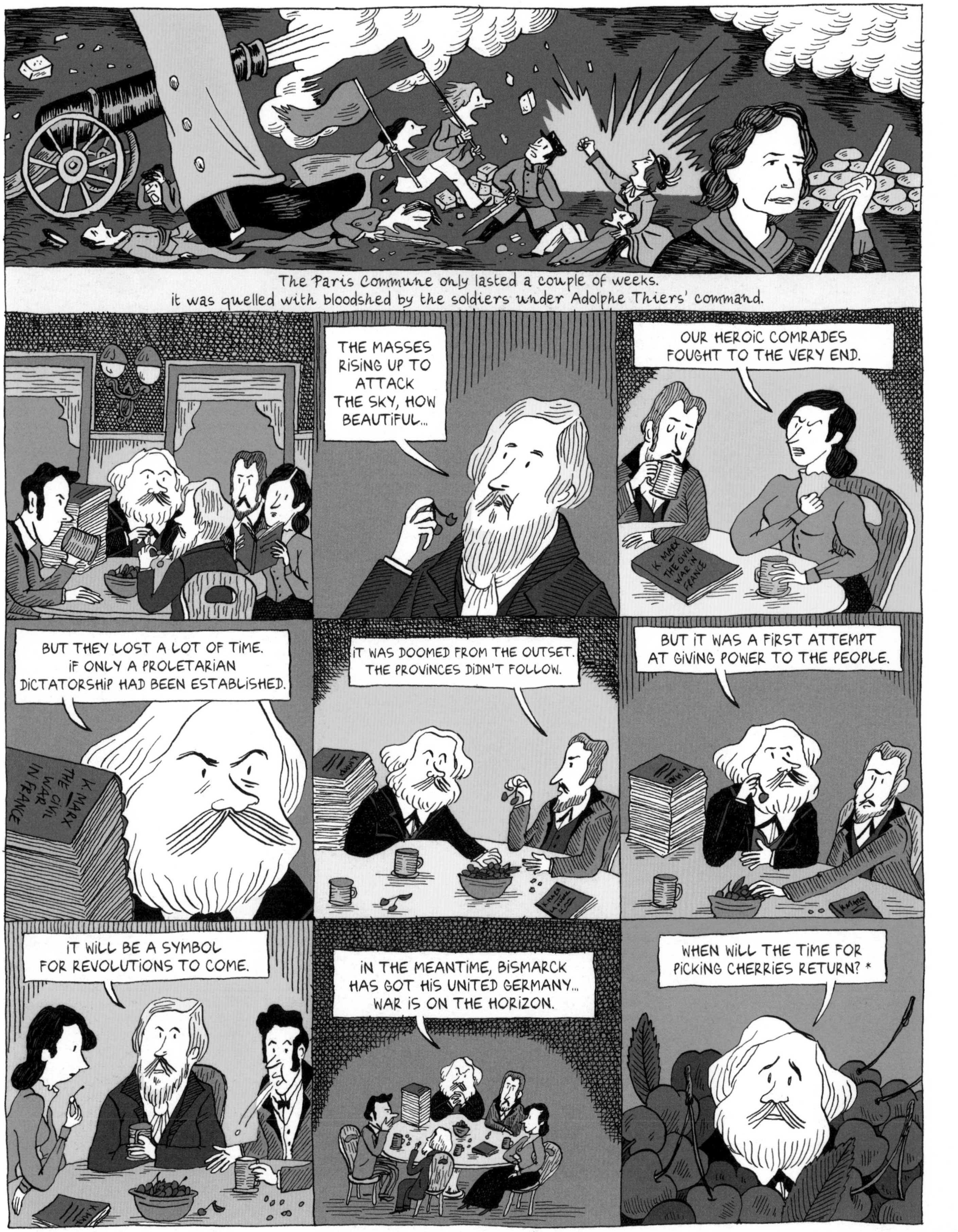
The Paris Commune only lasted a couple of weeks.
it was quelled with bloodshed by the soldiers under Adolphe Thiers' command.
THE MASSES RISING UP TO ATTACK THE SKY, HOW BEAUTIFUL...
OUR HEROIC COMRADES FOUGHT TO THE VERY END.
K MARX THE CIVIL WAR IN FRANCE
BUT THEY LOST A LOT OF TIME. IF ONLY A PROLETARIAN DICTATORSHIP HAD BEEN ESTABLISHED.
K. MARX THE CIVIL WAR IN FRANCE
IT WAS DOOMED FROM THE OUTSET. THE PROVINCES DIDN'T FOLLOW.
BUT IT WAS A FIRST ATTEMPT AT GIVING POWER TO THE PEOPLE.
IT WILL BE A SYMBOL FOR REVOLUTIONS TO COME.
IN THE MEANTIME, BISMARCK HAS GOT HIS UNITED GERMANY... WAR IS ON THE HORIZON.
WHEN WILL THE TIME FOR PICKING CHERRIES RETURN? *

*Reference to "Le Temps des Cerises" a song written in 1866 strongly associated with the Paris Commune.

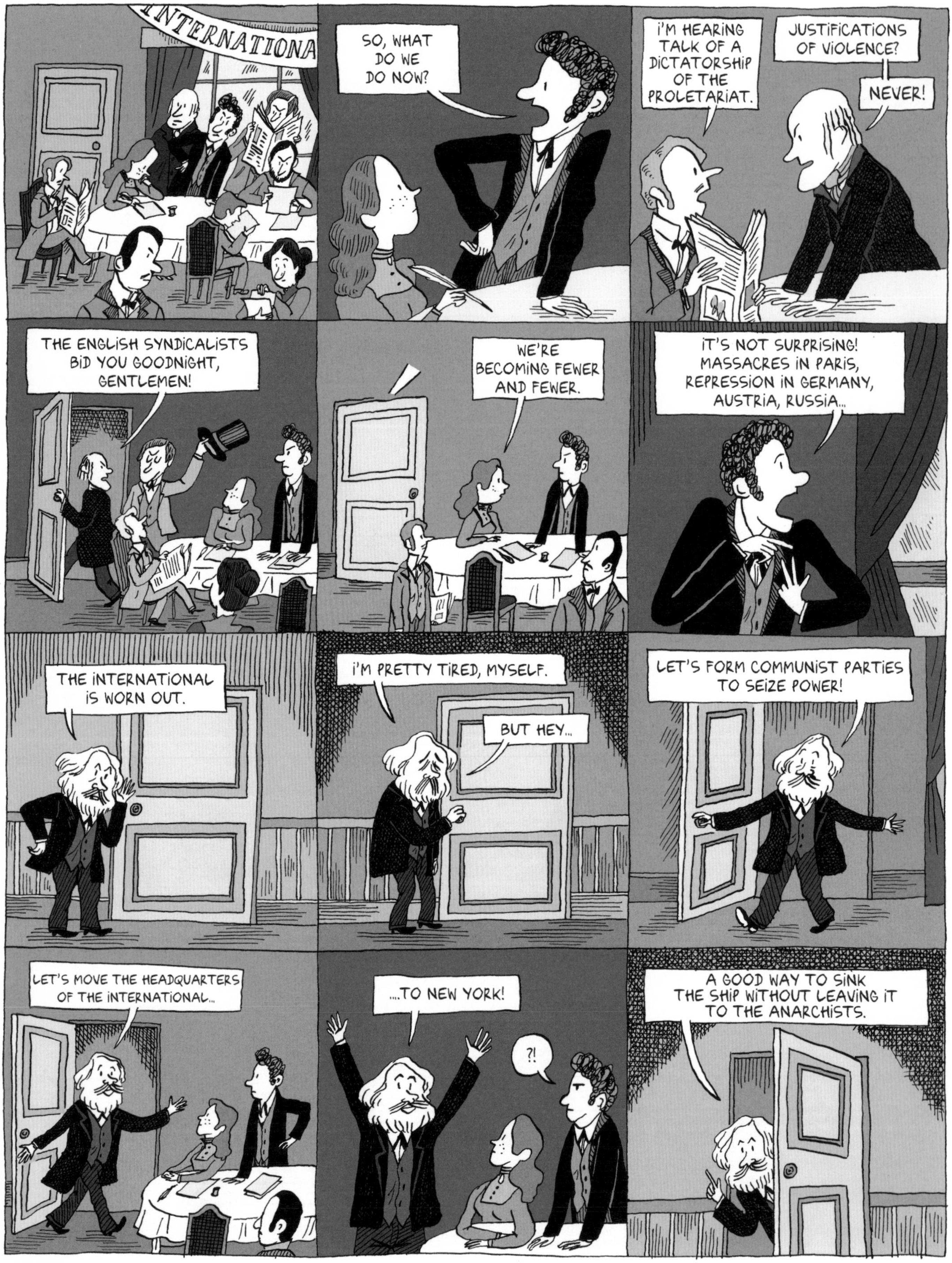
INTERNATIONA
SO, WHAT DO WE DO NOW?
I'M HEARING TALK OF A DICTATORSHIP OF THE PROLETARIAT.
JUSTIFICATIONS OF VIOLENCE?
NEVER!
THE ENGLISH SYNDICALISTS BID YOU GOODNIGHT, GENTLEMEN!
WE'RE BECOMING FEWER AND FEWER.
IT'S NOT SURPRISING! MASSACRES IN PARIS, REPRESSION IN GERMANY, AUSTRIA, RUSSIA...
THE INTERNATIONAL IS WORN OUT.
I'M PRETTY TIRED, MYSELF.
BUT HEY...
LET'S FORM COMMUNIST PARTIES TO SEIZE POWER!
LET'S MOVE THE HEADQUARTERS OF THE INTERNATIONAL...
...TO NEW YORK!
?!
A GOOD WAY TO SINK THE SHIP WITHOUT LEAVING IT TO THE ANARCHISTS.

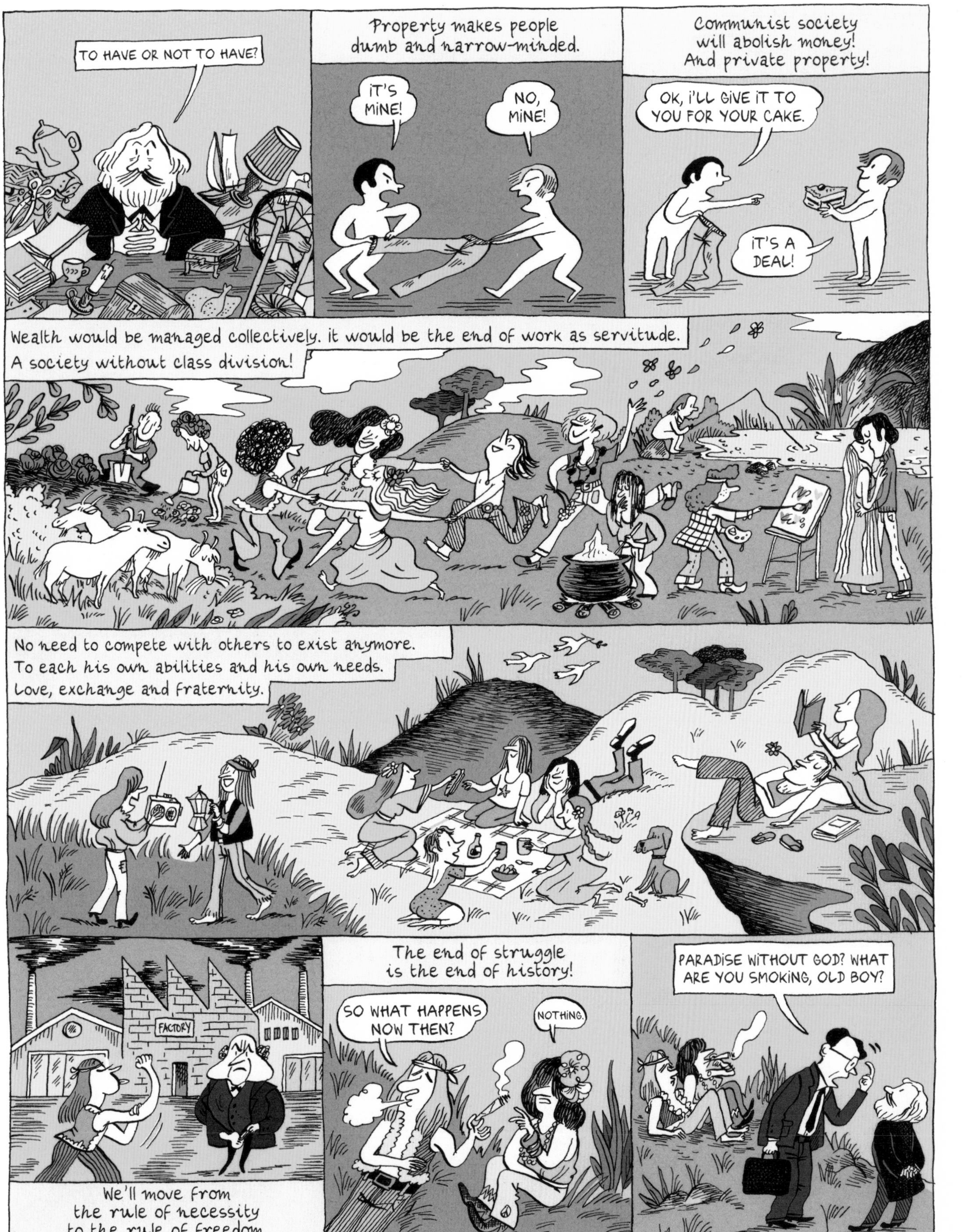
TO HAVE OR NOT TO HAVE?
Property makes people dumb and narrow-minded.
IT'S MINE!
NO, MINE!
Communist society will abolish money! And private property!
OK, I'LL GIVE IT TO YOU FOR YOUR CAKE.
IT'S A DEAL!
Wealth would be managed collectively. It would be the end of work as servitude.
A society without class division!
No need to compete with others to exist anymore.
To each his own abilities and his own needs.
Love, exchange and fraternity.
FACTORY
We'll move from the rule of necessity to the rule of freedom.
The end of struggle is the end of history!
SO WHAT HAPPENS NOW THEN?
NOTHING.
PARADISE WITHOUT GOD? WHAT ARE YOU SMOKING, OLD BOY?

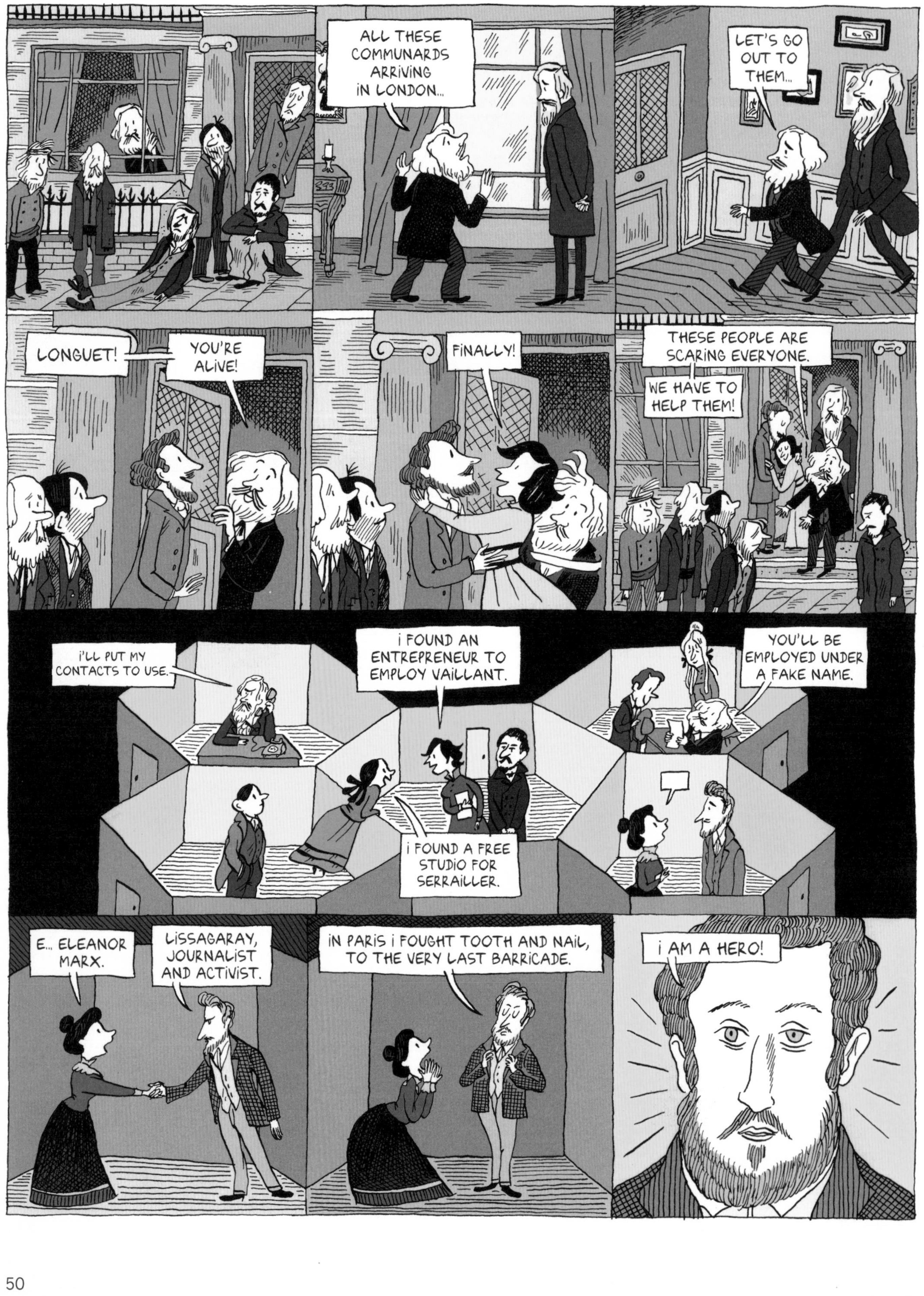
ALL THESE COMMUNARDS ARRIVING IN LONDON...
LET'S GO OUT TO THEM...
LONGUET!
YOU'RE ALIVE!
FINALLY!
THESE PEOPLE ARE SCARING EVERYONE.
WE HAVE TO HELP THEM!
I'LL PUT MY CONTACTS TO USE.
I FOUND AN ENTREPRENEUR TO EMPLOY VAILLANT.
YOU'LL BE EMPLOYED UNDER A FAKE NAME.
I FOUND A FREE STUDIO FOR SERRAILLER.
E... ELEANOR MARX.
LISSAGARAY, JOURNALIST AND ACTIVIST.
IN PARIS I FOUGHT TOOTH AND NAIL, TO THE VERY LAST BARRICADE.
I AM A HERO!

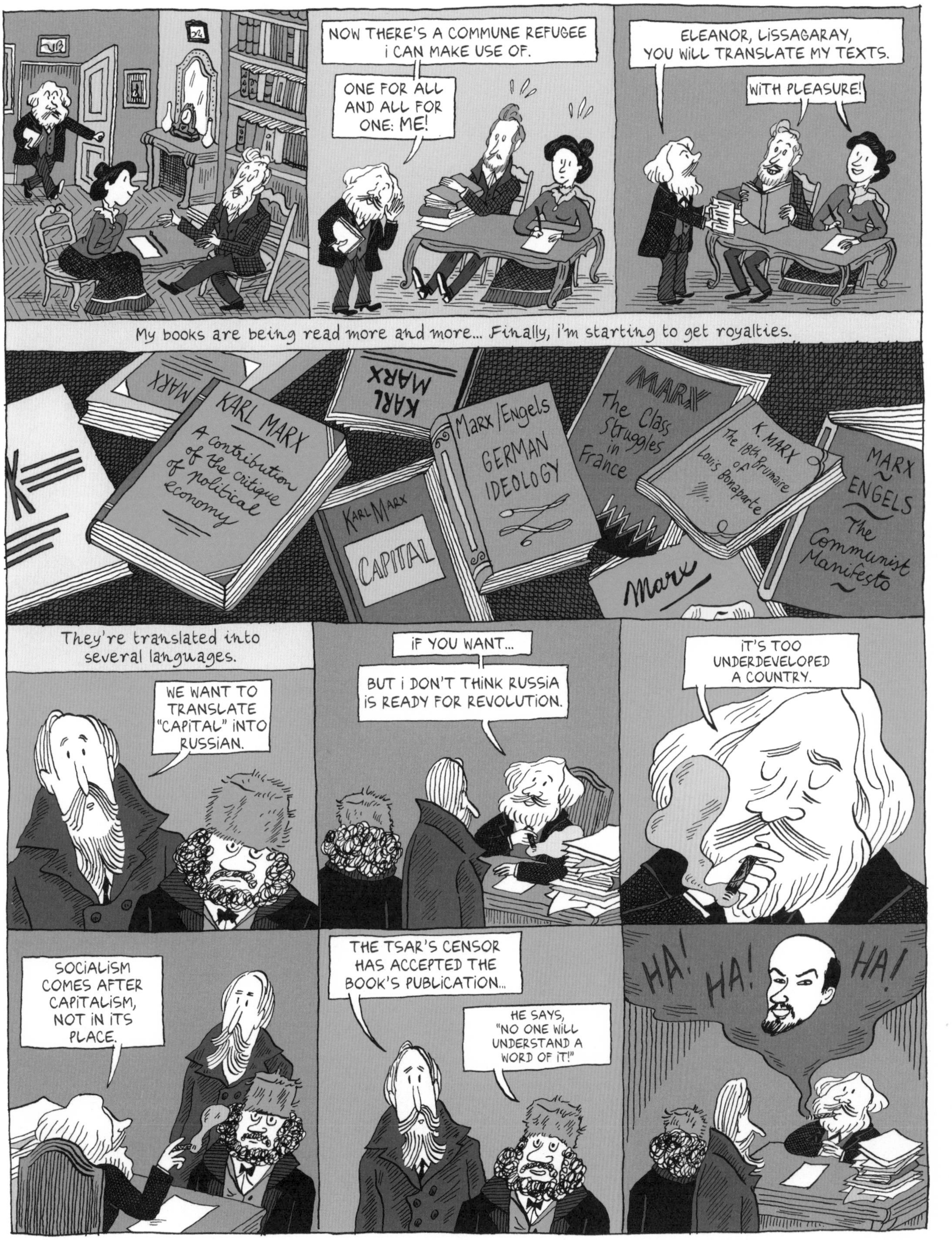
NOW THERE'S A COMMUNE REFUGEE I CAN MAKE USE OF.
ONE FOR ALL AND ALL FOR ONE: ME!
ELEANOR, LISSAGARAY, YOU WILL TRANSLATE MY TEXTS.
WITH PLEASURE!
My books are being read more and more... Finally, I'm starting to get royalties.
KARL MARX
KARL MARX A contribution of the critique of political economy
Marx/Engels GERMAN IDEOLOGY
MARX The Class Struggles in France
K. MARX The 18th Brumaire of Louis Bonaparte
MARX ENGELS The Communist Manifesto
KARL MARX CAPITAL
Marx
They're translated into several languages.
WE WANT TO TRANSLATE "CAPITAL" INTO RUSSIAN.
IF YOU WANT...
BUT I DON'T THINK RUSSIA IS READY FOR REVOLUTION.
IT'S TOO UNDERDEVELOPED A COUNTRY.
SOCIALISM COMES AFTER CAPITALISM, NOT IN ITS PLACE.
THE TSAR'S CENSOR HAS ACCEPTED THE BOOK'S PUBLICATION...
HE SAYS, "NO ONE WILL UNDERSTAND A WORD OF IT!"
HA! HA! HA!

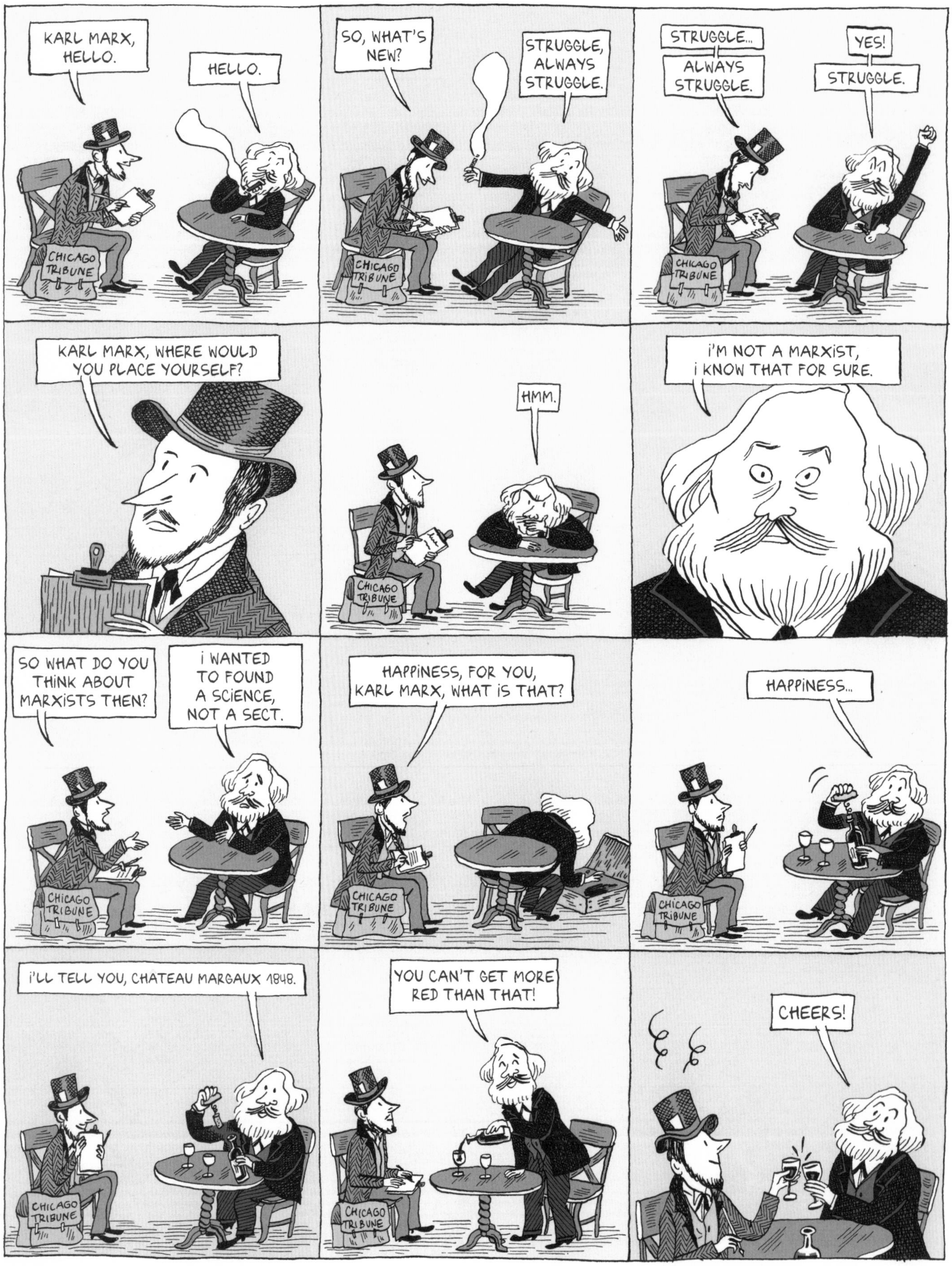
KARL MARX, HELLO.
HELLO.
CHICAGO TRIBUNE
SO, WHAT'S NEW?
STRUGGLE, ALWAYS STRUGGLE.
CHICAGO TRIBUNE
STRUGGLE...
ALWAYS STRUGGLE.
YES!
STRUGGLE.
CHICAGO TRIBUNE
KARL MARX, WHERE WOULD YOU PLACE YOURSELF?
HMM.
CHICAGO TRIBUNE
I'M NOT A MARXIST, I KNOW THAT FOR SURE.
SO WHAT DO YOU THINK ABOUT MARXISTS THEN?
I WANTED TO FOUND A SCIENCE, NOT A SECT.
CHICAGO TRIBUNE
HAPPINESS, FOR YOU, KARL MARX, WHAT IS THAT?
CHICAGO TRIBUNE
HAPPINESS...
CHICAGO TRIBUNE
I'LL TELL YOU, CHATEAU MARGAUX 1848.
CHICAGO TRIBUNE
YOU CAN'T GET MORE RED THAN THAT!
CHICAGO TRIBUNE
CHEERS!

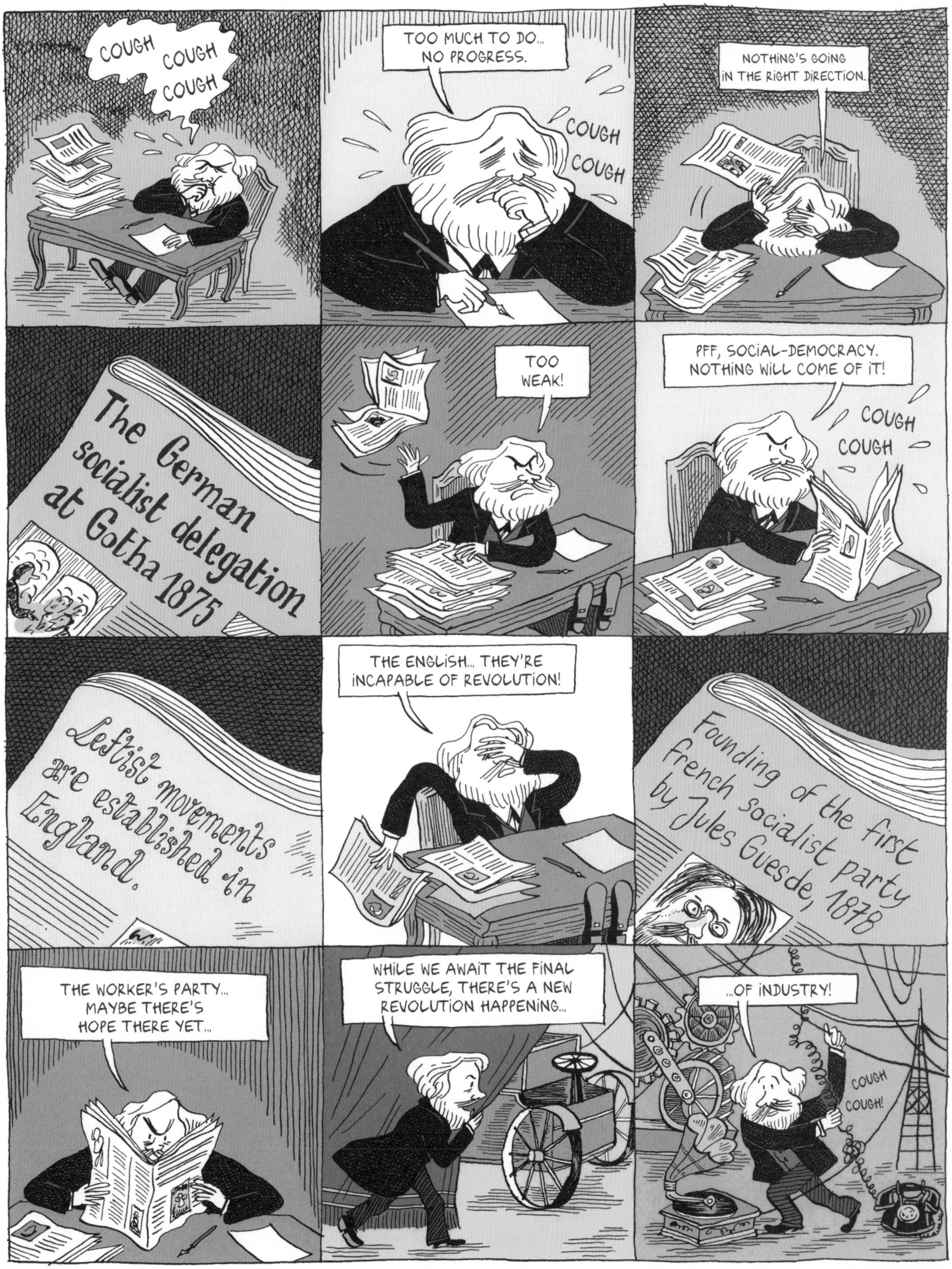
COUGH COUGH COUGH
TOO MUCH TO DO... NO PROGRESS.
COUGH COUGH
NOTHING'S GOING IN THE RIGHT DIRECTION.
The German socialist delegation at Gotha 1875
TOO WEAK!
PFF, SOCIAL-DEMOCRACY. NOTHING WILL COME OF IT!
COUGH COUGH
Leftist movements are established in England.
THE ENGLISH... THEY'RE INCAPABLE OF REVOLUTION!
Founding of the first french socialist party by Jules Guesde, 1878
THE WORKER'S PARTY... MAYBE THERE'S HOPE THERE YET...
WHILE WE AWAIT THE FINAL STRUGGLE, THERE'S A NEW REVOLUTION HAPPENING...
...OF INDUSTRY!
COUGH COUGH!

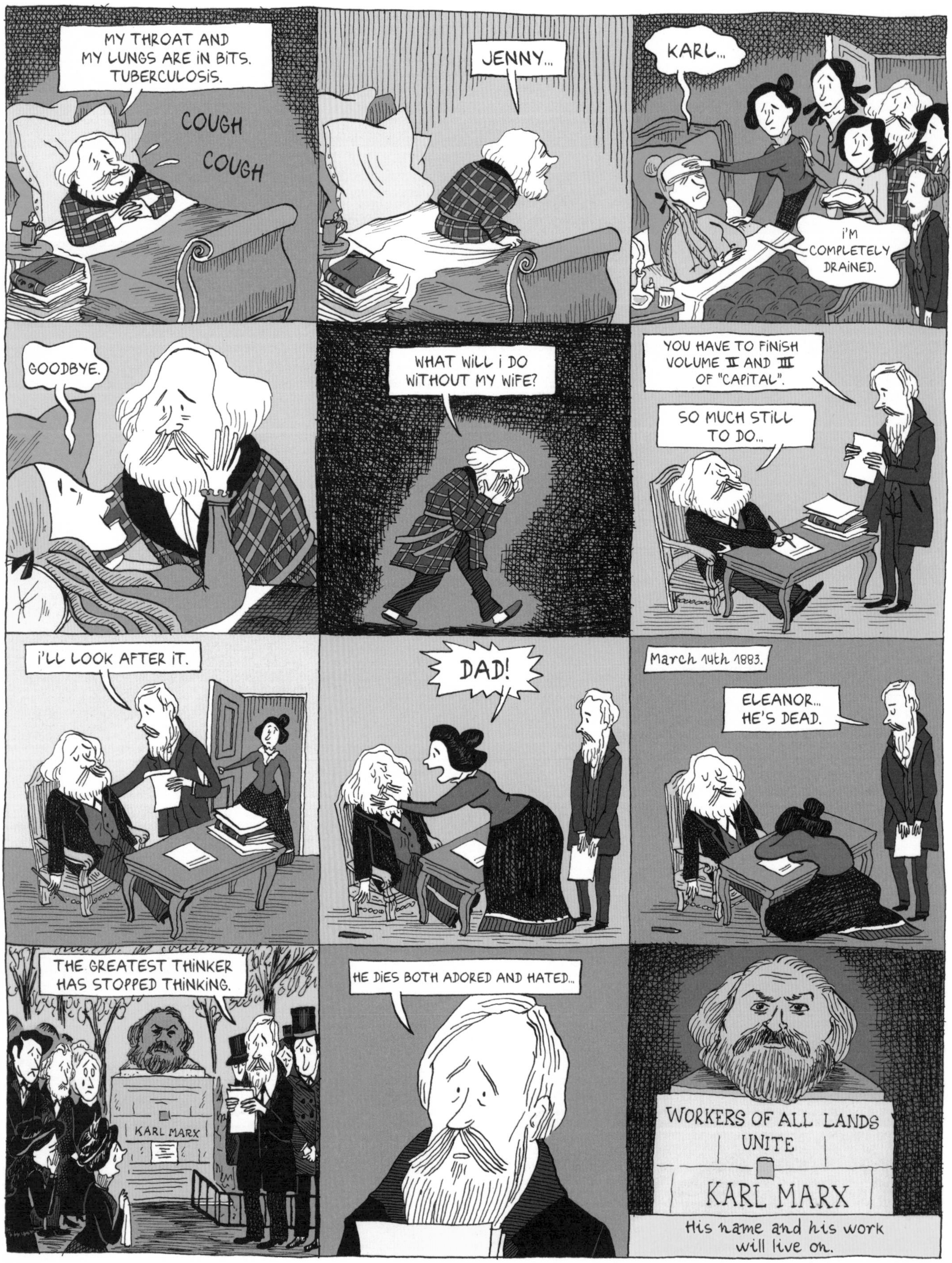
MY THROAT AND MY LUNGS ARE IN BITS. TUBERCULOSIS.
COUGH
COUGH
JENNY...
KARL...
I'M COMPLETELY DRAINED.
GOODBYE.
WHAT WILL I DO WITHOUT MY WIFE?
YOU HAVE TO FINISH VOLUME II AND III OF "CAPITAL".
SO MUCH STILL TO DO...
I'LL LOOK AFTER IT.
DAD!
March 14th 1883.
ELEANOR... HE'S DEAD.
THE GREATEST THINKER HAS STOPPED THINKING.
KARL MARX
HE DIES BOTH ADORED AND HATED...
WORKERS OF ALL LANDS UNITE
KARL MARX
His name and his work will live on.

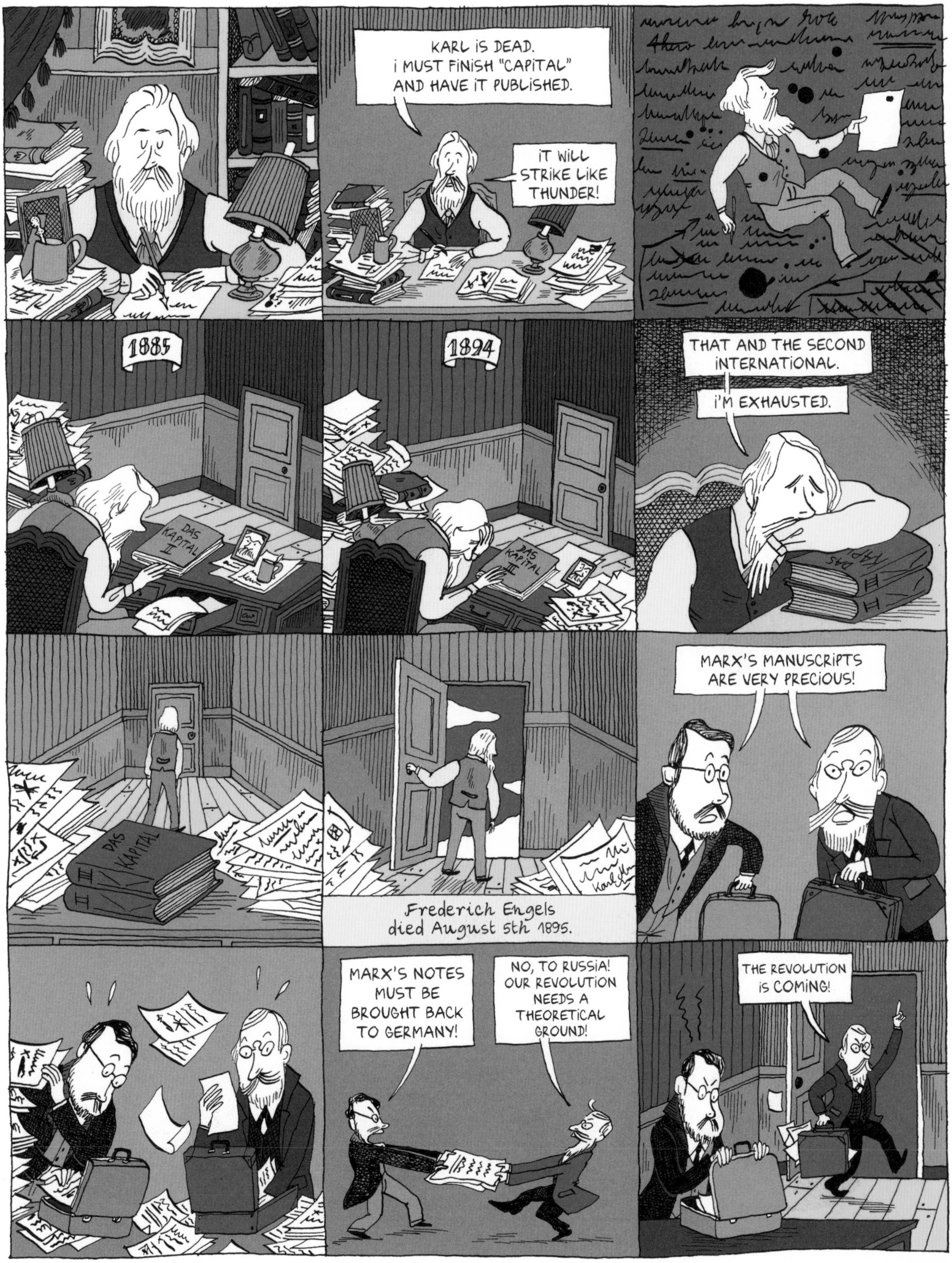
KARL IS DEAD. I MUST FINISH "CAPITAL" AND HAVE IT PUBLISHED.
IT WILL STRIKE LIKE THUNDER!
1885
DAS KAPITAL II
1894
DAS KAPITAL III
THAT AND THE SECOND INTERNATIONAL.
I'M EXHAUSTED.
DAS KAPITAL
Frederich Engels died August 5th 1895.
MARX'S MANUSCRIPTS ARE VERY PRECIOUS!
MARX'S NOTES MUST BE BROUGHT BACK TO GERMANY!
NO, TO RUSSIA! OUR REVOLUTION NEEDS A THEORETICAL GROUND!
THE REVOLUTION IS COMING!

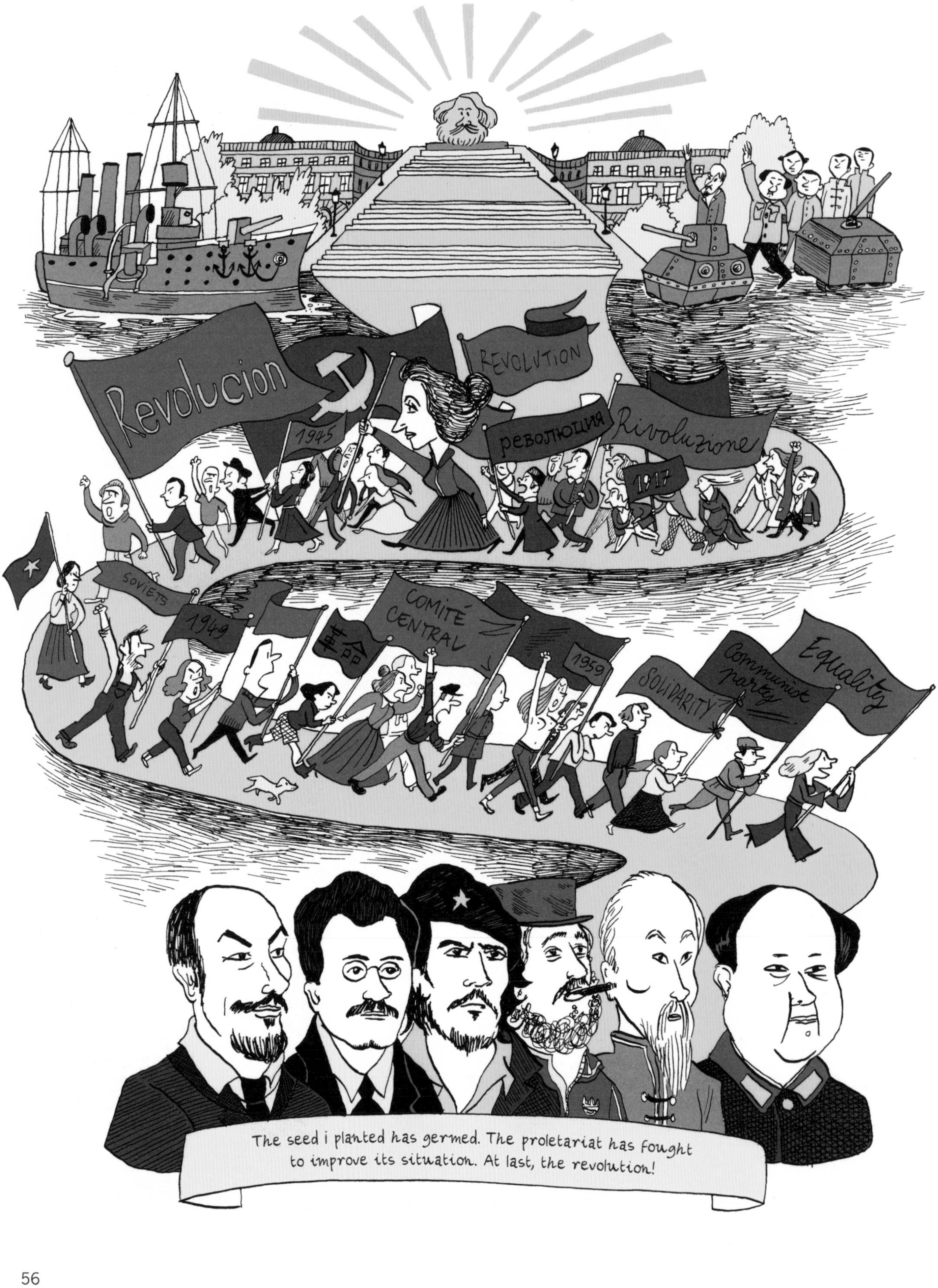
Revolucion
REVOLUTION
1945
революция
Rivoluzione
1917
SOVIETS
1949
革命
COMITÉ CENTRAL
1959
SOLIDARITY
Communist party
Equality
The seed i planted has germed. The proletariat has fought to improve its situation. At last, the revolution!

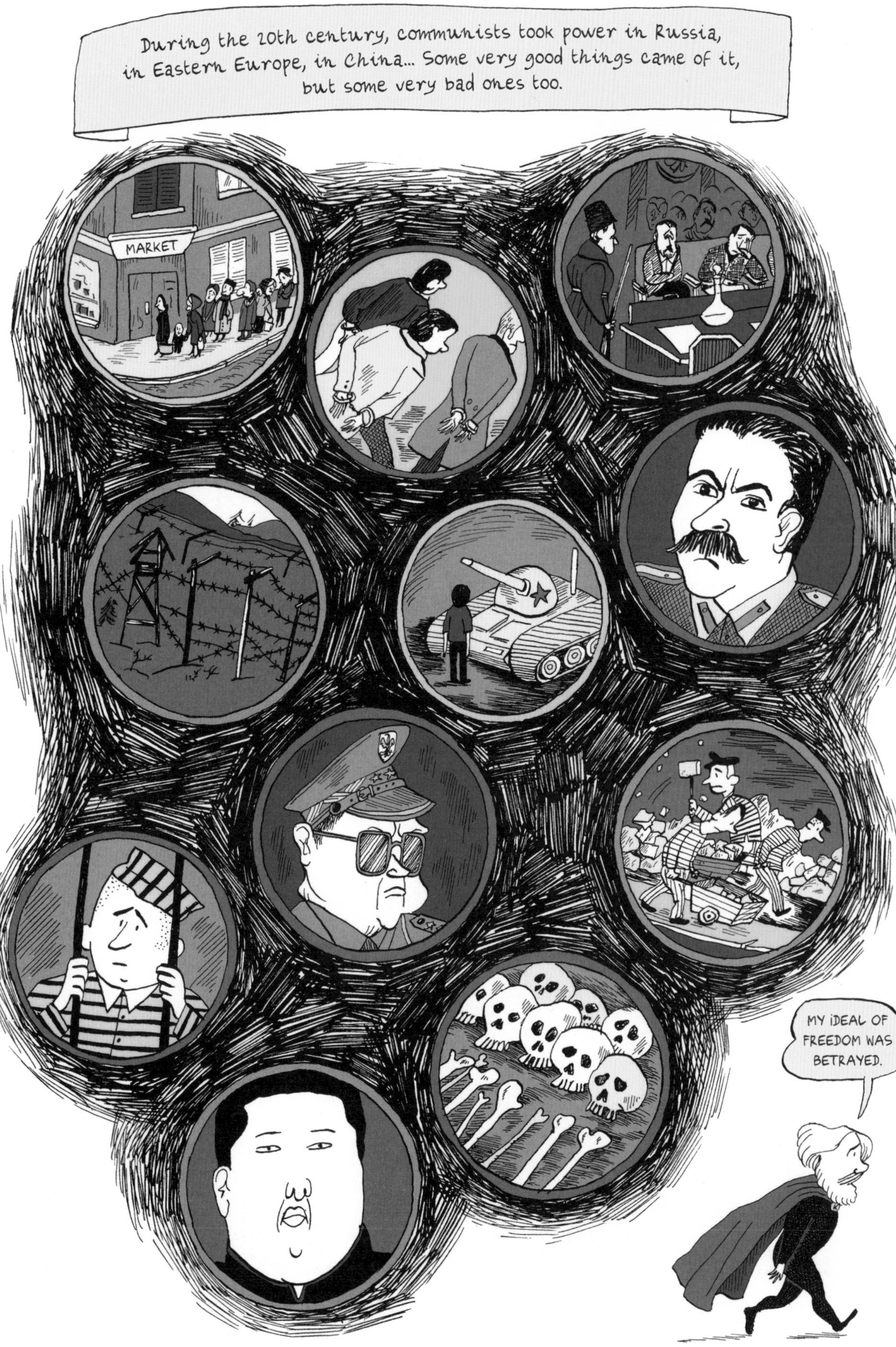
During the 20th century, communists took power in Russia, in Eastern Europe, in China... Some very good things came of it, but some very bad ones too.
MARKET
MY IDEAL OF FREEDOM WAS BETRAYED.

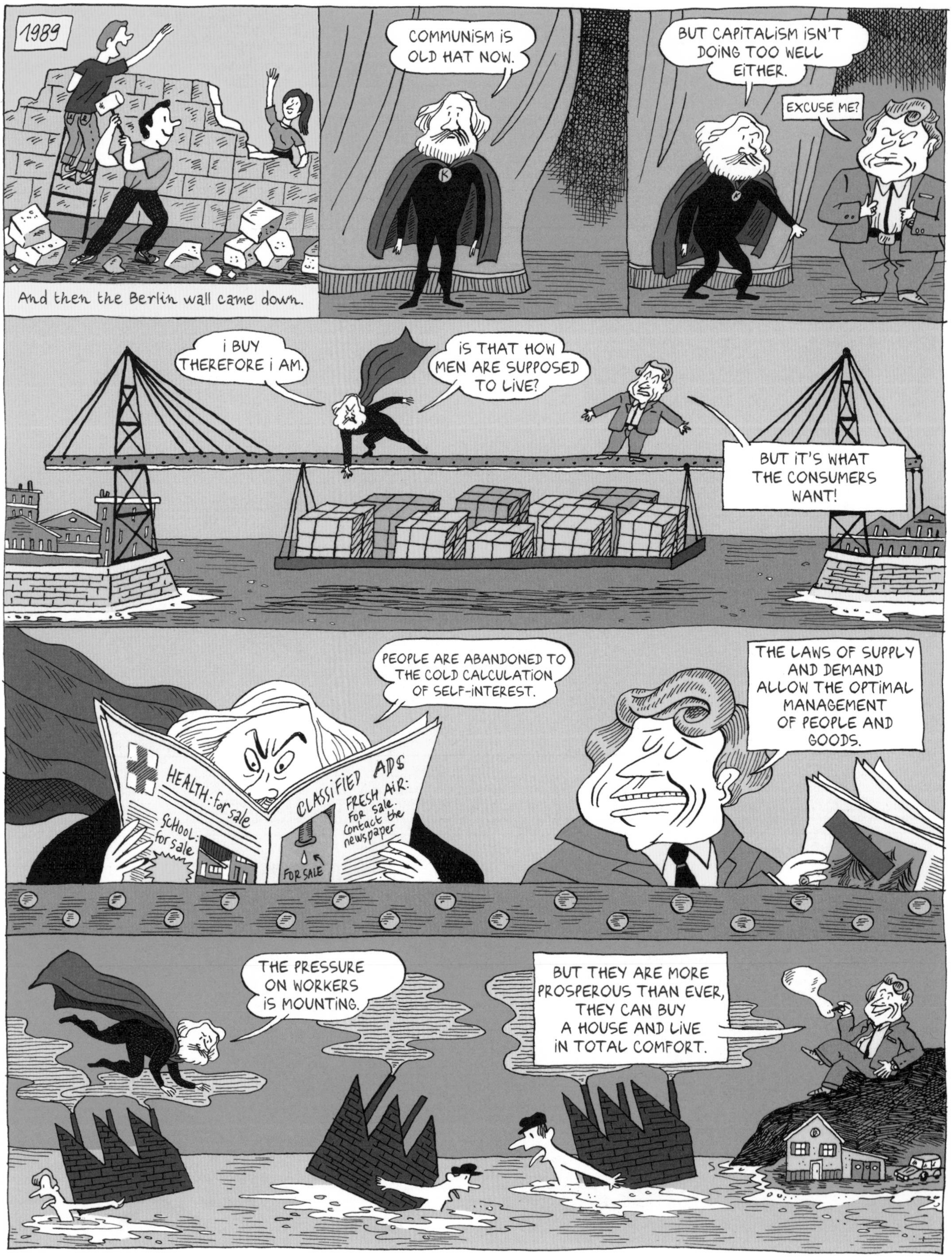

1989
And then the Berlin wall came down.
COMMUNISM IS OLD HAT NOW.
BUT CAPITALISM ISN'T DOING TOO WELL EITHER.
EXCUSE ME?
I BUY THEREFORE I AM.
IS THAT HOW MEN ARE SUPPOSED TO LIVE?
BUT IT'S WHAT THE CONSUMERS WANT!
PEOPLE ARE ABANDONED TO THE COLD CALCULATION OF SELF-INTEREST.
HEALTH: for sale
CLASSIFIED ADS
FRESH AIR: For sale. Contact the newspaper
SCHOOL: for sale
FOR SALE
THE LAWS OF SUPPLY AND DEMAND ALLOW THE OPTIMAL MANAGEMENT OF PEOPLE AND GOODS.
THE PRESSURE ON WORKERS IS MOUNTING.
BUT THEY ARE MORE PROSPEROUS THAN EVER, THEY CAN BUY A HOUSE AND LIVE IN TOTAL COMFORT.

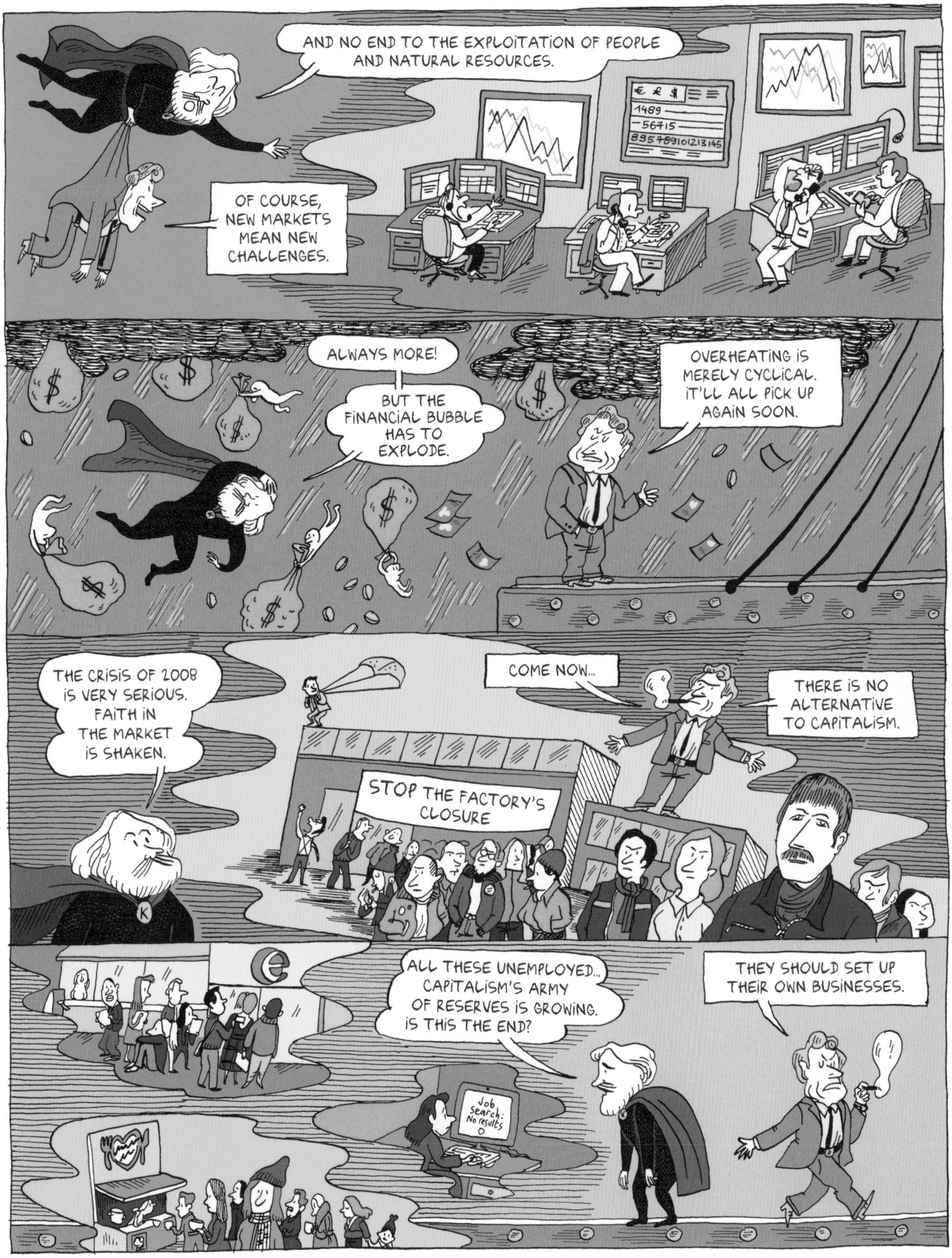
AND NO END TO THE EXPLOITATION OF PEOPLE AND NATURAL RESOURCES.
OF COURSE, NEW MARKETS MEAN NEW CHALLENGES.
€ £ $
1489
56715
ALWAYS MORE!
BUT THE FINANCIAL BUBBLE HAS TO EXPLODE.
OVERHEATING IS MERELY CYCLICAL. IT'LL ALL PICK UP AGAIN SOON.
THE CRISIS OF 2008 IS VERY SERIOUS. FAITH IN THE MARKET IS SHAKEN.
STOP THE FACTORY'S CLOSURE
COME NOW...
THERE IS NO ALTERNATIVE TO CAPITALISM.
ALL THESE UNEMPLOYED... CAPITALISM'S ARMY OF RESERVES IS GROWING. IS THIS THE END?
Job search: No results
THEY SHOULD SET UP THEIR OWN BUSINESSES.

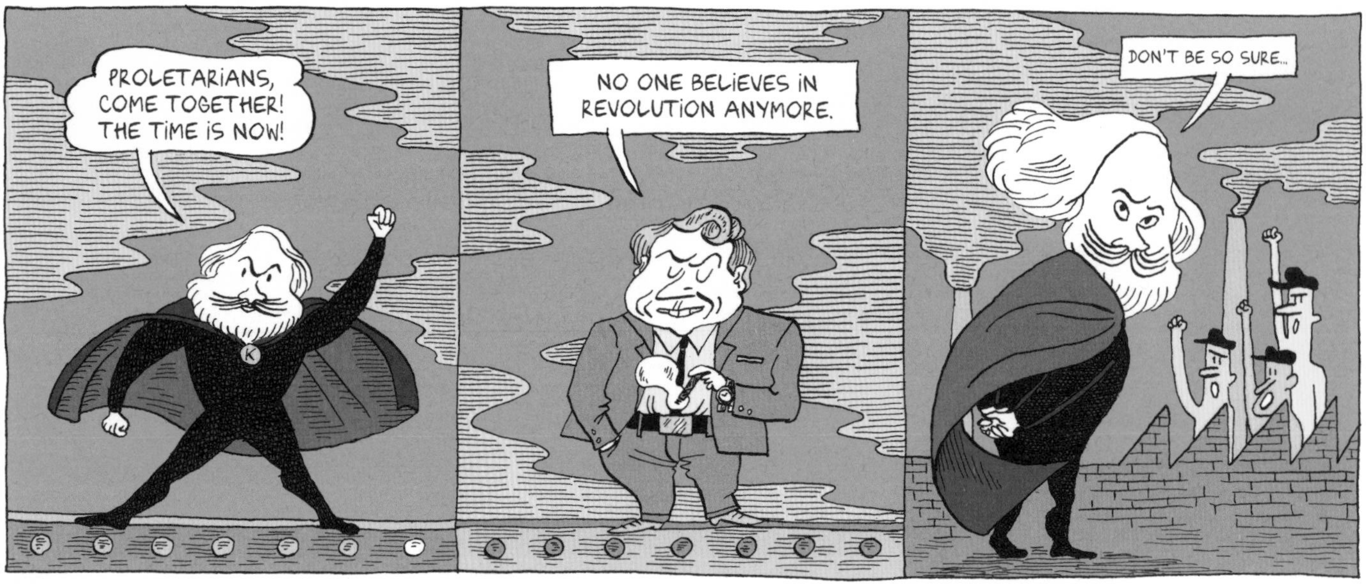
PROLETARIANS, COME TOGETHER! THE TIME IS NOW!
NO ONE BELIEVES IN REVOLUTION ANYMORE.
DON'T BE SO SURE...

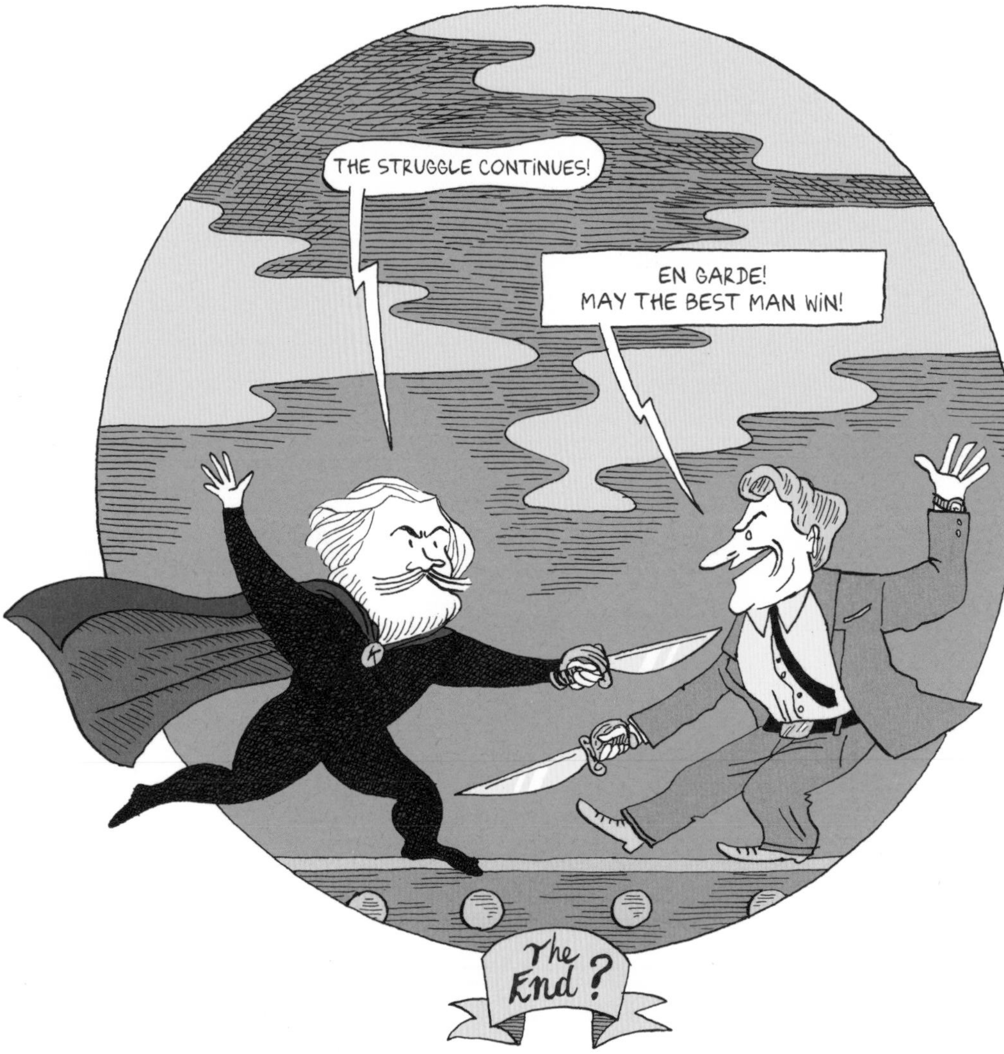
THE STRUGGLE CONTINUES!
EN GARDE! MAY THE BEST MAN WIN!
The End?

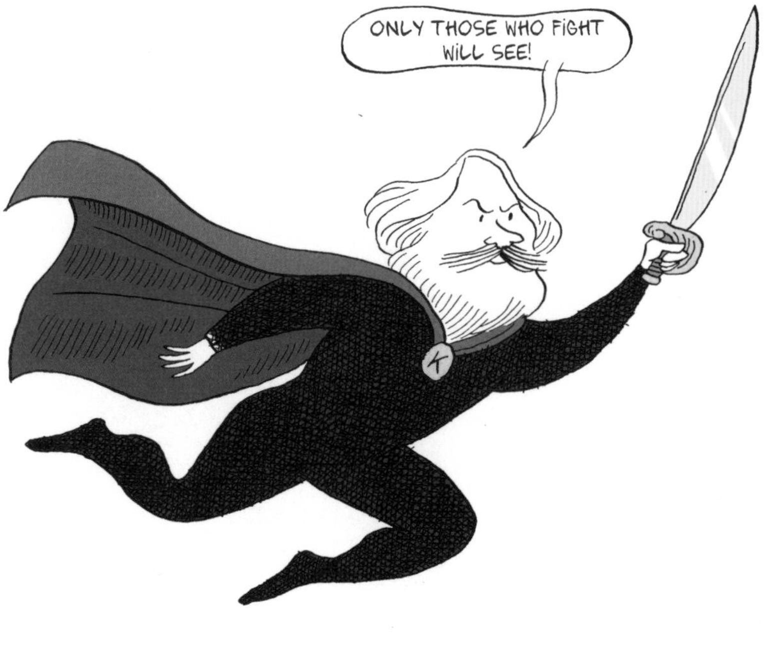
ONLY THOSE WHO FIGHT WILL SEE!

A SELECTION OF MARX TEXTS

On the Jewish Question (1844)
A Contribution to the Critique of Hegel's Philosophy of Right (1844)
Theses on Feuerbach (1845)

WITH ENGELS

The Germany ideology (1846)
The Communist Manifesto (1848)
A Contribution to the Critique of Political Economy (1859)
Capital (volume i, 1867, volumes ii and iii are posthumous
and have been published thanks to Engels.)

ABOUT FRANCE:

The Class Struggles in France (1850)
The 18th Brumaire of Louis Bonaparte (1852)
The Civil War in France (1871)

ALSO BY CORINNE MAIER AND ANNE SIMON

FREUD, AN ILLUSTRATED BIOGRAPHY